How to stop gambling

Quit gambling and save yourself from addiction

How to stop gambling by Lucky Willis

Copyright

Except in the case of a brief citation embodied in critical reviews and certain other commercial uses permitted by brand law, no part of this publication may be reproduced, distributed, or transmitted in any form or by any means, including photocopying, recording, or other electronic or mechanical styles, without the publisher's prior written authorization.

How to stop gambling by Lucky Willis

Table of Contents

Introduction
Chapter 1: Understanding Gambling Addiction
Types of Gambling Disorders
The Psychology of Gambling
Recognizing the Signs and Symptoms
Chapter 2: The Impact of Gambling Addiction
Financial Implications
Effects on Relationships
Impact on Career and Daily Life
Chapter 3: Identifying Your Triggers
Personal Reflection: Recognizing Your Triggers
Managing and Avoiding Triggers
Chapter 4: Developing a Recovery Mindset
Setting Realistic Goals
Building Self-Awareness
Cultivating Resilience
Chapter 5: Seeking Professional Help
Finding the Right Therapist or Counselor
The Role of Support Groups
Chapter 6: Self-Help Strategies
Mindfulness and Meditation
Journaling and Reflection
Cognitive Behavioral Techniques
Chapter 7: Building a Support Network
Joining Support Groups
Online Communities and Resources
Maintaining Supportive Relationships
Chapter 8: Financial Recovery and Management

How to stop gambling by Lucky Willis

Creating a Financial Plan
Avoiding Financial Triggers
Seeking Financial Counseling
Chapter 9: Healthy Alternatives to Gambling
Physical Activities and Sports
Creative Outlets
Volunteering and Community Service
Chapter 10: Preventing Relapse
Strategies to Prevent Relapse
Dealing with Relapse if it Occurs
Learning from Setbacks
Chapter 11: Long-Term Recovery and Maintenance
Ongoing Self-Improvement
Continual Learning and Growth
Staying Engaged in Recovery
Integrating Self-Improvement Practices
Embracing Continual Learning and Growth
Chapter 12: Inspiring Stories of Recovery
Real-Life Stories of Overcoming Gambling Addiction
Lessons Learned from Others
Lessons Learned from Others
Your Journey to Recovery
Conclusion

Introduction

Understanding Gambling Addiction

Gambling addiction, also known as compulsive gambling or gambling disorder, is a behavioral addiction characterized by the inability to resist the impulse to gamble, despite the harmful consequences it may bring to one's life. Unlike casual gambling, where individuals can engage in the activity for fun or social reasons, gambling addiction takes control of the person's life, leading to severe emotional, financial, and social repercussions.

The nature of gambling addiction lies in its ability to stimulate the brain's reward system, much like drugs or alcohol. This stimulation often results in a euphoric feeling, leading to repeated behavior in an attempt to recreate that high. Over time, the individual may require more frequent and higher-stakes gambling to achieve the same pleasure, leading to a downward spiral of dependency and loss of control.

Several factors contribute to the development of gambling addiction, including genetic, environmental, and psychological influences. For some, a family history of addiction may increase their susceptibility. Others may turn to gambling as a way to escape from stress, anxiety, or depression, only to find themselves trapped in a cycle of addiction.

Recognizing gambling addiction can be challenging, as individuals often go to great lengths to hide their behavior. Some common signs include an increasing preoccupation with gambling, lying to loved ones about the extent of their gambling, and experiencing withdrawal symptoms such as irritability or restlessness when not gambling.

The Purpose of This Book

The primary aim of this book is to provide comprehensive guidance and support to individuals struggling with gambling addiction. While the journey to recovery is deeply personal and can be fraught with challenges, this book seeks to offer practical strategies, insights, and encouragement to help readers regain control over their lives.

By delving into the psychological, emotional, and social aspects of gambling addiction, this book aims to equip readers with a thorough understanding of their condition. This knowledge is crucial, as it empowers individuals to recognize their triggers, understand the underlying causes of their addiction, and implement effective coping mechanisms.

Additionally, this book seeks to address the stigma often associated with gambling addiction. Many individuals suffering from this condition feel a sense of shame or guilt, which can prevent them from seeking help. By sharing personal stories of recovery and highlighting the experiences of others who have faced similar struggles, this book aims to foster a sense of community and hope.

Ultimately, the purpose of this book is to serve as a beacon of hope and a practical resource for anyone ready to take the first step towards recovery. It is designed to be a companion on the journey to overcoming gambling addiction, providing support and guidance every step of the way.

How to Use This Book

This book is structured to provide a step-by-step approach to overcoming gambling addiction, making it a valuable tool for both individuals struggling with the condition and their loved ones. Each chapter is dedicated to a specific aspect of the recovery process, offering detailed explanations, practical advice, and actionable steps.

Here's how you can make the most of this book:

1. **Read at Your Own Pace**: Recovery is a personal journey, and everyone moves at their own pace. Feel free to read through the chapters in order, or skip to sections that resonate with your current needs.

2. **Utilize the Resources**: Each chapter includes a list of additional resources such as websites, support groups, and hotlines. These resources can provide additional support and information as you work towards recovery.

3. **Keep a Journal**: Consider keeping a journal as you read through this book. Documenting your thoughts, feelings, and progress can be a powerful tool in your recovery journey.

4. **Seek Support**: While this book provides valuable guidance, it is also important to seek support from professionals and support groups. Don't hesitate to reach out for help when needed.

5. **Revisit Chapters as Needed**: Recovery is not always a linear process. You may find it helpful to revisit certain chapters or exercises as you progress in your journey.

By following this approach, you can maximize the benefits of this book and take meaningful steps towards overcoming gambling addiction.

Chapter 1: Understanding Gambling Addiction

What is Gambling Addiction?

Gambling addiction, also known as pathological gambling, compulsive gambling, or gambling disorder, is a condition characterized by the inability to control the urge to gamble, even when it leads to negative consequences. This addiction is recognized by the American Psychiatric Association and is included in the Diagnostic and Statistical Manual of Mental Disorders (DSM-5) under the category of substance-related and addictive disorders. Gambling addiction can affect anyone, regardless of age, gender, or social status, and it often leads to severe personal, financial, and social repercussions.

The nature of gambling addiction is complex, involving both psychological and physiological components. At its core, gambling addiction is driven by the brain's reward system. When an individual gambles, the brain releases dopamine, a neurotransmitter associated with pleasure and reward. This release creates a feeling of euphoria, similar to the high experienced from drugs or alcohol. Over time, the individual becomes reliant on this feeling, leading to compulsive behavior as they chase the high.

One of the most challenging aspects of gambling addiction is that it is often hidden. Unlike substance abuse, where physical signs can be apparent, gambling addiction can be concealed, sometimes for years. People with gambling addiction may go to great lengths to hide their behavior, lying to loved ones and themselves about the extent of their problem.

The impact of gambling addiction is far-reaching. Financial ruin is common, with individuals often accumulating significant debt, losing their savings, and even engaging in illegal activities to fund their gambling. Relationships suffer as trust is eroded, and emotional and psychological health deteriorates, leading to depression, anxiety, and, in some cases, suicidal thoughts.

Understanding the complexities of gambling addiction is the first step in addressing and overcoming this condition. It requires a multi-faceted approach, involving psychological support, financial counseling, and, in many cases, medical intervention. Recognizing the signs and seeking help early can significantly improve the chances of recovery.

Types of Gambling Disorders

Gambling disorders can manifest in various forms, each with its unique characteristics and challenges. Understanding the different types of gambling disorders can help in identifying the specific nature of an individual's addiction and tailoring the appropriate treatment approach. Here are some common types of gambling disorders:

1. **Action Gambling**: This type of gambling disorder is characterized by the individual's preference for skill-based games, such as poker or sports betting. Action gamblers are often thrill-seekers who enjoy the excitement and competition of these games. They believe they can develop strategies and skills to win, which can lead to a sense of control over their gambling. However, this belief is often misplaced, as the outcomes of these games are still largely influenced by chance.

2. **Escape Gambling**: Escape gamblers use gambling as a way to numb emotional pain, stress, or trauma. They may prefer games that require less skill and more chance, such as slot machines or bingo. For escape gamblers, the act of gambling provides temporary relief from their problems, creating a cycle of dependency as they seek to avoid their underlying issues.

3. **Binge Gambling**: Binge gamblers may not gamble frequently, but when they do, they engage in intense, high-stakes sessions. These binges can lead to significant financial losses in a short period. Binge gamblers often experience periods of control where they abstain from gambling, only to relapse into destructive behavior when they start again.

4. **Problem Gambling**: Problem gambling is a broader category that includes any gambling behavior that disrupts an individual's life, but may not meet the full criteria for a gambling disorder. Problem gamblers may still experience significant negative consequences, such as financial difficulties or strained relationships, but their behavior may be less severe or less frequent than those with a full-blown gambling disorder.

5. **Compulsive Gambling**: Also known as pathological gambling, this is the most severe form of gambling disorder. Compulsive gamblers have an uncontrollable urge to gamble, regardless of the negative consequences. They often gamble to escape from problems, chase their losses, and lie about their gambling behavior. Compulsive gambling is a chronic condition that requires professional treatment to overcome.

6. **Internet Gambling Disorder**: With the rise of online gambling platforms, internet gambling disorder has become increasingly prevalent. This type of disorder involves compulsive use of online gambling sites,

including virtual casinos, sports betting websites, and online poker rooms. The accessibility and anonymity of online gambling can exacerbate the addiction, making it harder to control.

7. **Secondary Gambling Disorder**: This type of gambling disorder occurs in individuals who have another primary addiction or mental health disorder, such as substance abuse or depression. The gambling behavior may develop as a coping mechanism or as a result of the impaired judgment associated with their primary condition. Treatment for secondary gambling disorder often requires addressing both the gambling behavior and the underlying condition.

Understanding these different types of gambling disorders is crucial for identifying the specific nature of an individual's addiction and developing an effective treatment plan. Each type of disorder may require different therapeutic approaches and support systems to achieve recovery.

The Psychology of Gambling

The psychology of gambling is a complex and multifaceted field that explores the mental processes and emotional states that drive gambling behavior. Several psychological factors contribute to the development and perpetuation of gambling addiction, including cognitive biases, emotional regulation, and social influences. Understanding these factors can provide valuable insights into why individuals gamble and how to address their addiction effectively.

1. **Cognitive Biases**: Cognitive biases are systematic errors in thinking that affect the decisions and judgments people make. In the context of gambling, several cognitive biases can contribute to addictive behavior:

   - **The Gambler's Fallacy**: This is the belief that past events can influence future outcomes in a game of chance. For example, a gambler may believe that if a roulette wheel has landed on red several times in a row, it is more likely to land on black in the next spin. In reality, each spin is independent, and previous outcomes do not affect future results.

   - **Illusion of Control**: This bias occurs when gamblers believe they have more control over the outcome of a game than they actually do. For instance, a gambler may think that their skills or strategies can influence the outcome of a slot machine, which is purely a game of chance.

   - **Near-Miss Effect**: The near-miss effect refers to the phenomenon where near-wins (e.g., getting two out of three matching symbols on a slot machine) are perceived as almost winning, which can increase the motivation to continue gambling. This effect can create a false sense of hope and persistence in gambling behavior.

How to stop gambling by Lucky Willis

2. **Emotional Regulation**: Gambling can serve as a way to manage or escape from negative emotions such as stress, anxiety, or depression. For some individuals, gambling provides a temporary distraction or relief from emotional pain. However, this coping mechanism can quickly become maladaptive, leading to a cycle of addiction as individuals continue to gamble to avoid dealing with their underlying emotional issues.

3. **Reinforcement and Reward**: Gambling activates the brain's reward system by releasing dopamine, a neurotransmitter associated with pleasure and reinforcement. The intermittent and unpredictable nature of gambling rewards can make them particularly reinforcing. This pattern of occasional wins and frequent losses creates a variable ratio reinforcement schedule, which is known to be highly addictive. The anticipation of a potential win can be as powerful as the win itself, driving continued gambling behavior.

4. **Social Influences**: Social factors also play a significant role in gambling behavior. Peer pressure, cultural attitudes towards gambling, and the influence of family members who gamble can all contribute to the development of gambling addiction. Additionally, the social environment of gambling venues, such as casinos or online gambling communities, can create a sense of belonging and excitement that reinforces gambling behavior.

5. **Personality Traits**: Certain personality traits may make individuals more susceptible to gambling addiction. These traits include impulsivity, sensation-seeking, and a tendency to seek immediate gratification. Individuals with high levels of these traits may be more likely to engage in risky behaviors, including gambling.

6. **Psychological Comorbidities**: Gambling addiction often co-occurs with other psychological disorders, such as depression, anxiety, or substance abuse. These comorbidities can complicate the treatment of gambling addiction and may require integrated approaches that address both the gambling behavior and the underlying psychological issues.

Understanding the psychology of gambling is essential for developing effective interventions and treatment strategies. By addressing the cognitive biases, emotional regulation issues, and social influences that contribute to gambling addiction, individuals can develop healthier coping mechanisms and make more informed decisions about their gambling behavior.

Recognizing the Signs and Symptoms

Recognizing the signs and symptoms of gambling addiction is crucial for early intervention and effective treatment. Gambling addiction can manifest in various ways, affecting an individual's emotional, financial, social, and psychological well-being. Here are some common signs and symptoms of gambling addiction:

1. **Preoccupation with Gambling**: Individuals with gambling addiction often spend a significant amount of time thinking about gambling. They may frequently plan their next gambling session, think about past gambling experiences, or fantasize about future wins. This preoccupation can interfere with daily activities and responsibilities.

2. **Increasing Bets**: Over time, individuals with gambling addiction may find that they need to gamble with increasing amounts of money to achieve the same level of excitement or pleasure. This phenomenon, known as tolerance, can lead to more significant financial losses and higher-risk behaviors.

3. **Chasing Losses**: One of the hallmark signs of gambling addiction is the tendency to chase losses. After losing money, individuals may continue to gamble in an attempt to win back what they have lost. This behavior often leads to a cycle of escalating losses and increased desperation.

4. **Inability to Stop Gambling**: Despite repeated attempts to cut back or stop gambling, individuals with gambling addiction often find themselves unable to control their behavior. They may make promises to themselves or others to stop gambling, only to break those promises and continue gambling.

5. **Lying and Deception**: To conceal the extent of their gambling behavior, individuals with gambling addiction may lie to family members, friends, or therapists. They may also engage in deceptive behaviors, such as hiding bills, receipts, or bank statements that show gambling transactions.

6. **Financial Problems**: Gambling addiction often leads to severe financial difficulties. Individuals may deplete their savings, accumulate significant debt, or even resort to borrowing money or engaging in illegal activities to fund their gambling. The financial strain can also lead to problems paying bills, rent, or mortgage payments.

7. **Neglecting Responsibilities**: As gambling takes up more time and energy, individuals may begin to neglect their responsibilities at work, school, or home. They may miss important deadlines, perform poorly at their job, or neglect household chores and family obligations.

8. **Emotional and Psychological Symptoms**: Gambling addiction can take a toll on an individual's emotional and psychological well-being. Common

symptoms include anxiety, depression, irritability, and mood swings. Some individuals may also experience feelings of guilt, shame, or hopelessness related to their gambling behavior.

9. **Relationship Problems**: The impact of gambling addiction on relationships can be profound. Individuals may experience conflicts with family members, friends, or romantic partners due to their gambling behavior. Trust issues, arguments, and emotional distance are common problems in relationships affected by gambling addiction.

10. **Withdrawal Symptoms**: When individuals with gambling addiction attempt to cut back or stop gambling, they may experience withdrawal symptoms. These symptoms can include restlessness, irritability, insomnia, and difficulty concentrating. The discomfort of withdrawal can drive individuals back to gambling as a way to relieve these symptoms.

11. **Using Gambling as an Escape**: Individuals with gambling addiction often use gambling as a way to escape from problems or negative emotions. They may gamble to avoid dealing with stress, anxiety, depression, or other personal issues. This behavior can create a cycle of dependency, where gambling becomes a primary coping mechanism.

12. **Failed Attempts to Stop**: Despite recognizing the negative consequences of their behavior, individuals

How to stop gambling by Lucky Willis

with gambling addiction often make multiple unsuccessful attempts to stop or reduce their gambling. These failed attempts can lead to feelings of helplessness and despair.

Recognizing these signs and symptoms is the first step in addressing gambling addiction. Early intervention can significantly improve the chances of successful recovery. If you or someone you know is exhibiting these symptoms, it is important to seek help from a healthcare professional, counselor, or support group specializing in gambling addiction. Treatment options are available, and recovery is possible with the right support and strategies.

Chapter 2: The Impact of Gambling Addiction

Emotional and Mental Health Consequences

Gambling addiction exerts a profound impact on an individual's emotional and mental well-being, often leading to a cascade of negative consequences that affect every aspect of their life. Understanding these consequences is crucial for recognizing the severity of gambling addiction and addressing its effects effectively.

1. **Depression and Anxiety**: Many individuals with gambling addiction experience symptoms of depression and anxiety. The stress of financial losses, guilt over deceptive behavior, and the inability to stop gambling can contribute to feelings of hopelessness and despair. These mental health issues may worsen as the addiction progresses, creating a vicious cycle where gambling serves as a temporary escape from negative emotions.

2. **Low Self-Esteem**: Gambling addiction can erode self-esteem and self-worth. Individuals may feel ashamed of their behavior, especially if they have lied or deceived loved ones to hide their gambling activities. This sense of guilt and self-blame can further exacerbate feelings of inadequacy and contribute to a negative self-image.

3. **Mood Swings and Irritability**: Fluctuations in mood are common among individuals with gambling addiction. The highs of winning can be followed by deep lows after losses, leading to mood swings and emotional instability. Irritability and agitation may also occur, especially when individuals are unable to gamble or are facing consequences related to their addiction.

4. **Suicidal Thoughts and Behaviors**: The emotional turmoil caused by gambling addiction can lead to suicidal thoughts and behaviors. Feelings of desperation, overwhelming debt, and a sense of being trapped in a cycle of addiction can drive individuals to consider or attempt suicide as a way to escape their problems. It is crucial for individuals experiencing suicidal thoughts to seek immediate help from mental health professionals or support services.

5. **Sleep Disturbances**: Difficulty sleeping or insomnia is another common consequence of gambling addiction. The stress and anxiety associated with financial losses or gambling-related problems can disrupt sleep patterns, leading to fatigue, irritability, and difficulty concentrating during the day.

6. **Psychological Disorders**: Gambling addiction often co-occurs with other psychological disorders, such as substance abuse, bipolar disorder, or obsessive-compulsive disorder (OCD). These comorbidities can complicate treatment and exacerbate the symptoms of both conditions. Integrated treatment

approaches that address both gambling addiction and underlying psychological disorders are essential for achieving long-term recovery.

Understanding the emotional and mental health consequences of gambling addiction highlights the need for comprehensive treatment approaches that address the underlying psychological issues contributing to the addiction. Effective treatment may include therapy, support groups, medication for co-occurring disorders, and strategies for coping with stress and negative emotions without resorting to gambling.

Financial Implications

One of the most devastating consequences of gambling addiction is its impact on financial stability and security. Individuals with gambling addiction often experience significant financial losses and may resort to desperate measures to fund their addiction. Understanding the financial implications of gambling addiction is essential for recognizing the severity of the problem and taking steps towards recovery.

1. **Debt and Financial Ruin**: Gambling addiction can lead to substantial debts, as individuals may borrow money, take out loans, or max out credit cards to finance their gambling habits. The financial losses incurred through gambling can quickly spiral out of control,

leaving individuals with overwhelming debt and no clear way to repay it.

2. **Legal and Criminal Issues**: In some cases, individuals with gambling addiction may engage in illegal activities, such as theft or fraud, to fund their gambling. Legal consequences can result from these actions, including criminal charges, fines, and imprisonment. Gambling addiction can also lead to civil legal issues, such as bankruptcy or lawsuits from creditors seeking repayment.

3. **Loss of Savings and Assets**: Individuals with gambling addiction may deplete their savings, liquidate assets, or sell valuable possessions to continue gambling or repay debts. This financial instability can jeopardize their future financial security and undermine their ability to meet basic needs, such as housing, food, and healthcare.

4. **Impact on Credit Rating**: Accumulating debt and defaulting on payments can damage an individual's credit rating. A poor credit score can make it difficult to secure loans, obtain housing or employment, and access financial services in the future. Rebuilding credit and financial stability may require years of diligent effort and responsible financial management.

5. **Financial Dependence and Burden on Others**: Gambling addiction can create financial dependence on family members, friends, or partners who may be

unaware of the extent of the problem. Individuals may borrow money from loved ones with the promise of repayment, only to use the funds for gambling or other expenses related to their addiction. This financial burden can strain relationships and lead to resentment and distrust.

6. **Bankruptcy and Foreclosure**: For some individuals, gambling addiction culminates in financial ruin, leading to bankruptcy, foreclosure, or repossession of assets. These legal and financial consequences can have long-lasting effects on an individual's financial stability, creditworthiness, and overall well-being.

Understanding the severe financial implications of gambling addiction underscores the importance of early intervention and comprehensive treatment. Financial counseling, debt management strategies, and responsible financial practices are essential components of recovery efforts aimed at restoring financial stability and independence.

Effects on Relationships

Gambling addiction can have devastating effects on relationships with family members, friends, romantic partners, and colleagues. The behavioral and emotional changes associated with gambling addiction can strain interpersonal connections and erode trust, often leading to profound and lasting consequences.

How to stop gambling by Lucky Willis

1. **Trust Issues**: Deceptive behavior, such as lying about gambling activities or financial losses, can erode trust in relationships. Loved ones may feel betrayed, hurt, or deceived by the individual's actions, leading to feelings of resentment and suspicion. Rebuilding trust can be a challenging and time-consuming process, requiring open communication and consistent honesty.

2. **Communication Breakdown**: Gambling addiction can disrupt healthy communication patterns within relationships. Individuals may withdraw emotionally, become defensive or secretive about their behavior, or avoid discussing their gambling addiction altogether. This breakdown in communication can hinder efforts to seek support, address underlying issues, and work towards recovery as a united front.

3. **Emotional Distance and Isolation**: The emotional strain of gambling addiction can create distance and isolation within relationships. Individuals may withdraw from social interactions, prioritize gambling over spending time with loved ones, or become emotionally unavailable due to preoccupation with their addiction. This isolation can exacerbate feelings of loneliness and alienation for both the individual with gambling addiction and their loved ones.

4. **Impact on Family Dynamics**: Gambling addiction can disrupt family dynamics and roles, leading to increased stress and conflict within the household. Family members may take on additional responsibilities,

such as managing finances or caring for children, as the individual with gambling addiction prioritizes gambling over family obligations. Children may be particularly vulnerable to the negative effects of gambling addiction, experiencing emotional distress, academic difficulties, and disruptions in their daily routines.

5. **Financial Strain**: The financial consequences of gambling addiction can strain relationships as individuals struggle to repay debts, manage household expenses, and maintain a stable standard of living. Arguments over money, budgeting, and financial priorities are common among couples and families affected by gambling addiction. Financial strain can exacerbate existing tensions and contribute to relationship breakdowns.

6. **Enabling Behavior**: Loved ones may unintentionally enable gambling addiction by providing financial support, covering up losses, or minimizing the severity of the problem. Enabling behavior can prolong the cycle of addiction, preventing the individual from confronting their behavior and seeking help. It is essential for loved ones to set boundaries, seek support for themselves, and encourage the individual with gambling addiction to engage in treatment.

7. **Impact on Children**: Children growing up in households affected by gambling addiction may experience emotional, psychological, and developmental challenges. They may witness parental

conflict, financial instability, and neglect as their parents prioritize gambling over their caregiving responsibilities. These adverse childhood experiences can have long-term consequences for children's well-being, academic performance, and social relationships.

Understanding the profound effects of gambling addiction on relationships underscores the importance of family therapy, support groups, and counseling for both individuals and their loved ones. Rebuilding trust, improving communication, and addressing underlying issues are essential steps towards healing and restoring healthy relationships.

Impact on Career and Daily Life

Gambling addiction can significantly impact an individual's career, academic pursuits, and daily functioning, leading to disruptions in productivity, performance, and personal well-being. Recognizing the impact of gambling addiction on career and daily life is essential for addressing the consequences and implementing strategies for recovery.

1. **Decline in Work Performance**: Individuals with gambling addiction may experience a decline in work performance due to preoccupation with gambling, emotional distress, and financial problems. They may miss deadlines, make mistakes, or have difficulty concentrating on tasks as their attention is diverted to gambling-related thoughts and activities.

2. **Attendance Issues**: Gambling addiction can lead to frequent absences from work or school, as individuals prioritize gambling over their professional or academic responsibilities. Chronic absenteeism can jeopardize job security, academic standing, and opportunities for career advancement.

3. **Financial Instability**: The financial consequences of gambling addiction can create instability in an individual's life, affecting their ability to cover basic living expenses, pay bills, and maintain a stable financial situation. Financial stress can contribute to anxiety, depression, and overall dissatisfaction with life.

4. **Legal and Ethical Concerns**: In some cases, gambling addiction may lead to legal issues or ethical dilemmas in the workplace. Individuals may engage in fraudulent activities, embezzlement, or theft to fund their gambling, resulting in criminal charges, disciplinary action, or termination of employment. Gambling addiction can undermine trust and integrity in professional settings, jeopardizing career prospects and professional relationships.

5. **Social Isolation and Withdrawal**: Gambling addiction can lead to social withdrawal and isolation as individuals prioritize gambling over social interactions, hobbies, and leisure activities. They may feel ashamed or embarrassed about their gambling behavior, leading

to feelings of loneliness and alienation from friends, family, and colleagues.

6. **Health and Well-being**: The stress and emotional turmoil associated with gambling addiction can take a toll on an individual's physical health and overall well-being. Poor sleep patterns, unhealthy eating habits, and neglect of self-care may contribute to physical health problems, such as fatigue, weight gain or loss, and compromised immune function.

7. **Loss of Opportunities**: Gambling addiction can limit an individual's ability to pursue educational opportunities, career goals, and personal aspirations. Financial constraints, legal issues, and interpersonal conflicts may prevent individuals from achieving their full potential and realizing their dreams.

8. **Impact on Family and Relationships**: The consequences of gambling addiction extend beyond the individual to affect their family members, friends, and loved ones. Relationship strain, financial instability, and emotional distress can create ripple effects that impact the well-being and quality of life of those closest to the individual with gambling addiction.

Addressing the impact of gambling addiction on career and daily life requires a holistic approach that includes therapy, financial counseling, vocational rehabilitation, and support from employers, educators,

How to stop gambling by Lucky Willis

and community resources. By addressing the underlying issues contributing to gambling addiction and implementing strategies for recovery, individuals can rebuild their lives, regain stability, and pursue meaningful goals and aspirations.

Chapter 3: Identifying Your Triggers

Common Triggers for Gambling

Identifying triggers for gambling is a crucial step in understanding the factors that contribute to addictive behavior. Triggers are stimuli or situations that prompt individuals to engage in gambling activities, often leading to cravings and compulsive behavior. By recognizing common triggers, individuals can develop strategies to manage and avoid these situations, reducing the risk of relapse and promoting long-term recovery.

1. **Emotional Triggers**:
   - **Stress**: Stress is one of the most significant emotional triggers for gambling. Many individuals use gambling as a way to escape or cope with stressors in their lives, seeking temporary relief or distraction from overwhelming emotions.
   - **Anxiety**: Feelings of anxiety or nervousness can trigger gambling as individuals seek to alleviate their discomfort or uncertainty. The excitement and unpredictability of gambling may provide a temporary sense of control or relief from anxious thoughts.

- **Depression**: Individuals experiencing depression may turn to gambling as a means of self-medication or to numb painful emotions. The thrill of gambling can temporarily lift mood or provide a distraction from feelings of sadness or hopelessness.

2. **Psychological Triggers**:
   - **Boredom**: Monotony or lack of stimulation can lead individuals to seek excitement and entertainment through gambling activities. The fast-paced nature of gambling games can provide a temporary thrill and alleviate feelings of boredom.
   - **Loneliness**: Feelings of loneliness or social isolation can trigger gambling as individuals seek companionship or connection in gambling venues or online communities. The social aspect of gambling can create a sense of belonging and camaraderie, albeit temporarily.

3. **Environmental Triggers**:
   - **Presence of Gambling Venues**: Physical proximity to casinos, gambling establishments, or online gambling platforms can act as environmental triggers for gambling. The availability and accessibility of gambling opportunities increase the likelihood of impulsive gambling behavior.
   - **Cues and Advertising**: Visual cues, such as advertisements, promotional offers, or gambling-related imagery, can trigger cravings and compulsive urges to gamble. These cues activate associative memories and emotions linked to past gambling experiences.

4. **Social Triggers**:
   - **Peer Influence**: Peer pressure or social norms surrounding gambling can influence individuals to participate in gambling activities. Social gatherings or events centered around gambling can normalize and encourage gambling behavior.
   - **Celebratory Occasions**: Festive occasions, celebrations, or special events may involve gambling as a form of entertainment or tradition. The social acceptance and excitement associated with these events can trigger gambling urges.

5. **Financial Triggers**:
   - **Financial Windfalls**: Sudden financial gains, such as bonuses, inheritance, or lottery winnings, can trigger gambling behavior as individuals seek to capitalize on their newfound wealth or experience a sense of invulnerability.
   - **Financial Hardship**: Financial difficulties, debt, or economic instability can trigger gambling as individuals attempt to alleviate financial stress or recover losses through gambling activities.

6. **Cognitive Triggers**:
   - **Availability Heuristic**: The availability heuristic is a cognitive bias where individuals assess the probability of an event based on how easily they can recall similar instances from memory. Past gambling wins or near-misses can create an illusion of control or likelihood of winning, triggering gambling behavior.

- **Optimism Bias**: Optimism bias is the tendency to overestimate the likelihood of positive outcomes and underestimate the probability of negative consequences. Individuals experiencing optimism bias may engage in gambling under the belief that they are more likely to win or that their luck will change.

Understanding these common triggers for gambling provides insight into the diverse factors that contribute to addictive behavior. Each individual may be susceptible to different triggers based on personal experiences, personality traits, and environmental influences. By identifying specific triggers that prompt gambling behavior, individuals can develop personalized strategies to manage cravings, reduce risk factors, and promote sustainable recovery.

Personal Reflection: Recognizing Your Triggers

Personal reflection is an essential component of identifying triggers for gambling addiction. It involves introspection, self-awareness, and honest assessment of one's thoughts, emotions, and behaviors related to gambling. By engaging in personal reflection, individuals can gain deeper insight into the underlying motivations and triggers that drive their gambling behavior, paving the way for meaningful change and recovery.

How to stop gambling by Lucky Willis

1. **Self-Assessment**: Begin by conducting a thorough self-assessment of your gambling habits, patterns, and triggers. Reflect on past gambling experiences, including when, where, and why you tend to gamble. Consider the emotional, psychological, and environmental factors that influence your decision to gamble.

2. **Journaling**: Keep a journal or diary to document your thoughts, feelings, and experiences related to gambling. Record instances when you felt the urge to gamble, the triggers that preceded these urges, and the outcomes of your gambling behavior. Writing can help clarify your thoughts, identify recurring patterns, and track your progress in managing triggers.

3. **Identifying Patterns**: Look for patterns or themes in your gambling behavior and triggers. Are there specific times of day, situations, or emotional states that consistently prompt you to gamble? Pay attention to cues, cravings, and automatic thoughts associated with gambling urges. Identifying patterns can empower you to anticipate triggers and implement effective coping strategies.

4. **Emotional Awareness**: Cultivate awareness of your emotions and their connection to gambling behavior. Notice how feelings of stress, boredom, loneliness, or excitement influence your desire to gamble. Practice mindfulness techniques, such as deep

breathing or meditation, to regulate emotions and reduce impulsivity in response to triggers.

5. **Behavioral Analysis**: Analyze your behaviors and responses in gambling-related situations. Consider how you typically react to triggers, such as reaching for your phone to access gambling apps or driving to a nearby casino. Recognize the chain of events leading up to gambling urges and identify alternative behaviors or distractions to interrupt this cycle.

6. **Self-Honesty and Accountability**: Be honest with yourself about the impact of gambling on your life, relationships, and well-being. Acknowledge any denial, rationalization, or minimization of your gambling behavior. Take responsibility for your actions and decisions, and commit to making positive changes to regain control over your gambling habits.

    Personal reflection requires courage, honesty, and self-awareness to confront challenging emotions and behaviors associated with gambling addiction. By gaining clarity on your triggers and motivations, you can empower yourself to make informed decisions, seek support, and take proactive steps towards recovery.

Managing and Avoiding Triggers

Effectively managing and avoiding triggers is essential for reducing the risk of relapse and maintaining long-term recovery from gambling addiction. By implementing proactive strategies and developing coping mechanisms, individuals can minimize exposure to triggers, strengthen resilience, and cultivate a supportive environment conducive to recovery.

1. **Identify High-Risk Situations**: Recognize situations, environments, or circumstances that commonly trigger gambling urges. Examples include passing by a casino, receiving a paycheck, experiencing stress at work, or socializing with friends who gamble. Identify specific cues and contexts that precede gambling behavior.

2. **Develop Coping Strategies**: Equip yourself with coping strategies to manage cravings and navigate high-risk situations effectively. Strategies may include:
   - **Mindfulness and Relaxation Techniques**: Practice mindfulness meditation, deep breathing exercises, or progressive muscle relaxation to reduce stress and regulate emotions.
   - **Distraction and Alternative Activities**: Engage in hobbies, physical exercise, creative pursuits, or social activities as healthy distractions from gambling urges.
   - **Positive Self-Talk**: Challenge negative thoughts and self-limiting beliefs associated with gambling.

Replace self-critical or defeatist thoughts with affirmations and empowering statements.
   - **Delay and Distract**: Delay acting on gambling urges by setting a timer or engaging in a different activity for a specified period. Use distraction techniques to redirect attention away from gambling thoughts.

3. **Modify Environments**: Modify your physical environment to minimize exposure to gambling triggers. Consider avoiding gambling venues, uninstalling gambling apps, or blocking access to gambling websites on your devices. Create a supportive home environment that promotes recovery and reduces temptation.

4. **Establish Support Systems**: Build a strong support network of family members, friends, peers, or support groups who understand your journey towards recovery. Seek encouragement, guidance, and accountability from individuals who prioritize your well-being and recovery goals.

5. **Develop a Relapse Prevention Plan**: Create a personalized relapse prevention plan outlining triggers, warning signs, and coping strategies to manage potential relapse situations. Review and revise your plan regularly to address emerging triggers and reinforce effective coping skills.

6. **Professional Support**: Seek professional support from therapists, counselors, or addiction specialists with experience in gambling addiction. Therapy sessions can

provide valuable insights, tools, and strategies for managing triggers, addressing underlying issues, and sustaining recovery.

Managing and avoiding triggers requires commitment, perseverance, and proactive effort to protect your recovery journey from gambling addiction. By implementing personalized strategies, seeking support, and prioritizing self-care, individuals can strengthen resilience, reduce vulnerability to triggers, and achieve sustainable recovery and well-being.

Chapter 3 explain the critical importance of identifying triggers for gambling addiction, understanding their impact, and developing effective strategies for managing and avoiding these triggers. By recognizing common triggers, engaging in personal reflection, and implementing proactive coping mechanisms, individuals can empower themselves to navigate challenges, reduce the risk of relapse, and sustain long-term recovery. Personalized strategies, support systems, and professional guidance play integral roles in promoting resilience, fostering positive change, and reclaiming control over gambling behaviors.

Chapter 4: Developing a Recovery Mindset

The Importance of Motivation

Motivation serves as a cornerstone for individuals recovering from gambling addiction, providing the driving force to initiate change, persevere through challenges, and sustain long-term recovery efforts. Understanding the dynamics of motivation within the context of gambling addiction is essential for cultivating a positive and resilient mindset conducive to recovery.

1. **Intrinsic vs. Extrinsic Motivation**:
   - **Intrinsic Motivation**: Intrinsic motivation arises from internal factors such as personal values, beliefs, and the inherent satisfaction derived from achieving personal goals. Individuals recovering from gambling addiction may be motivated by a desire for self-improvement, restoration of relationships, or reclaiming control over their lives.
   - **Extrinsic Motivation**: Extrinsic motivation stems from external factors such as rewards, recognition, or social approval. External incentives, such as financial stability, family support, or praise from others, can reinforce individuals' commitment to recovery and provide additional motivation to maintain positive behavioral changes.

2. **Stages of Change Model**:

How to stop gambling by Lucky Willis

- **Precontemplation**: Individuals in the precontemplation stage may not yet recognize or acknowledge the need for change regarding their gambling behavior. Motivational interventions aim to raise awareness of the consequences of gambling addiction and promote contemplation of behavior change.
- **Contemplation**: During the contemplation stage, individuals weigh the pros and cons of gambling cessation and consider the impact of their behavior on themselves and others. Motivation may fluctuate as individuals assess their readiness and willingness to commit to recovery efforts.
- **Preparation**: In the preparation stage, individuals actively plan and prepare for behavioral change, setting goals, seeking support, and developing coping strategies to manage triggers and cravings effectively.
- **Action**: The action stage involves implementing strategies and making concrete behavioral changes to reduce or eliminate gambling behavior. Motivation plays a crucial role in sustaining momentum, overcoming challenges, and maintaining adherence to recovery goals.
- **Maintenance**: Maintenance involves consolidating gains, preventing relapse, and integrating recovery behaviors into daily life. Motivation facilitates ongoing commitment to recovery, resilience in the face of setbacks, and the pursuit of long-term goals.

3. **Enhancing Motivation**:

- **Goal Setting**: Establish clear, specific, and achievable goals related to gambling cessation, financial stability, personal growth, and relationships. Setting short-term and long-term goals provides direction, fosters commitment, and enhances motivation to persevere through challenges.
- **Self-Efficacy**: Develop confidence in your ability to change gambling behavior and achieve recovery goals. Build self-efficacy through small successes, learning from setbacks, and recognizing personal strengths and capabilities.
- **Positive Reinforcement**: Acknowledge and celebrate progress, milestones, and achievements along the recovery journey. Positive reinforcement enhances motivation, reinforces desired behaviors, and promotes a sense of accomplishment and self-worth.
- **Support Systems**: Engage with supportive individuals, such as family members, friends, peers in recovery, or professional counselors. Social support provides encouragement, empathy, accountability, and practical assistance, bolstering motivation and resilience.

4. **Motivational Techniques and Strategies**:
- **Motivational Interviewing**: Utilize motivational interviewing techniques to explore ambivalence, enhance intrinsic motivation, and strengthen commitment to change. Empathetic listening, reflective questioning, and collaborative goal-setting facilitate a client-centered approach to recovery.

- **Visualization and Affirmations**: Use visualization techniques to imagine a future free from gambling addiction, visualizing goals achieved, and a fulfilling life. Affirmations reinforce positive beliefs, strengths, and intentions, promoting a proactive and optimistic mindset.
- **Education and Awareness**: Increase awareness of the impact of gambling addiction, potential consequences, and benefits of recovery. Education empowers individuals with knowledge, dispels myths, reduces stigma, and fosters informed decision-making regarding gambling behavior.

5. **Cognitive-Behavioral Strategies**: Incorporate cognitive-behavioral strategies, such as cognitive restructuring, problem-solving, and emotion regulation techniques. These strategies address distorted thinking patterns, manage stressors, and enhance coping skills essential for maintaining motivation and managing triggers.

6. **Resilience and Motivation**: Cultivate resilience as a foundational component of motivation in recovery from gambling addiction. Resilience enables individuals to adapt to adversity, bounce back from setbacks, and maintain a positive outlook despite challenges. Building resilience involves developing coping skills, fostering social connections, and cultivating self-care practices that promote emotional well-being and sustained motivation.

Setting Realistic Goals

Setting realistic and achievable goals is integral to the process of recovery from gambling addiction, providing individuals with a roadmap for change, a sense of direction, and motivation to pursue meaningful outcomes. By establishing clear goals, individuals can focus their efforts, track progress, and cultivate a sense of accomplishment and empowerment in their recovery journey.

1. **Types of Goals**:
   - **Short-term Goals**: Short-term goals are specific, measurable, and achievable objectives that individuals can accomplish within a relatively brief timeframe, such as one week or one month. Examples include attending a support group meeting, abstaining from gambling for a designated period, or practicing relaxation techniques daily.
   - **Long-term Goals**: Long-term goals are overarching objectives that individuals strive to achieve over an extended period, typically six months to a year or more. Examples include maintaining gambling abstinence, improving financial stability, repairing relationships, or pursuing vocational or educational aspirations.

2. **SMART Goals Framework**:
   - **Specific**: Clearly define the goal, including what you want to achieve, why it is important, and how you

will accomplish it. For example, "I will abstain from gambling for the next 30 days to regain control over my finances and prioritize my well-being."
   - **Measurable**: Establish criteria for measuring progress and success toward achieving the goal. Use quantifiable indicators, such as number of days abstinent from gambling, amount of money saved, or improvements in emotional well-being.
   - **Achievable**: Ensure that the goal is realistic and attainable given your current resources, capabilities, and circumstances. Set challenging yet feasible goals that stretch your abilities without overwhelming or discouraging you.
   - **Relevant**: Align the goal with your values, priorities, and long-term objectives in recovery from gambling addiction. Consider how achieving the goal contributes to your overall well-being, personal growth, and happiness.
   - **Time-bound**: Set a specific timeframe or deadline for achieving the goal, creating a sense of urgency and accountability. Establishing deadlines helps maintain focus, monitor progress, and celebrate achievements within a defined timeframe.

3. **Prioritizing Goals**:
   - **Immediate Needs**: Identify goals that address urgent or pressing concerns related to gambling addiction, such as abstaining from gambling, managing financial obligations, or repairing damaged relationships.
   - **Long-term Aspirations**: Prioritize goals that reflect your long-term vision for recovery and personal growth,

such as improving emotional well-being, pursuing educational or career goals, or rebuilding trust and intimacy in relationships.

4. **Breaking Down Goals**:
   - **Chunking**: Divide larger goals into smaller, manageable tasks or milestones to facilitate progress and prevent overwhelm. Focus on taking incremental steps toward achieving the overarching goal, celebrating achievements along the way.
   - **Action Plans**: Develop action plans outlining specific steps, resources, and timelines for achieving each goal. Identify potential obstacles or challenges and strategize proactive solutions to maintain motivation and momentum.

5. **Monitoring and Adjusting Goals**:
   - **Regular Evaluation**: Monitor your progress toward goals regularly, reflecting on achievements, challenges, and adjustments needed. Evaluate whether goals remain relevant, achievable, and aligned with your evolving needs and priorities in recovery.
   - **Flexibility**: Remain flexible and adaptive in revising goals based on changing circumstances, setbacks, or new insights gained in the recovery journey. Adjust timelines, strategies, or expectations as needed to promote continuous growth and resilience.

   Setting realistic goals empowers individuals recovering from gambling addiction to take proactive steps, build momentum, and achieve meaningful outcomes in their recovery journey. By leveraging the

SMART goals framework, prioritizing objectives, and fostering resilience, individuals can navigate challenges, celebrate successes, and sustain motivation toward long-term sobriety and well-being.

Building Self-Awareness

Self-awareness plays a pivotal role in the process of recovery from gambling addiction, fostering introspection, insight, and understanding of one's thoughts, emotions, behaviors, and motivations. By cultivating self-awareness, individuals can identify underlying triggers, recognize patterns of gambling behavior, and develop adaptive strategies for managing cravings and promoting lasting change.

1. **Definition of Self-Awareness**:
   - **Internal Reflection**: Engage in internal reflection and introspection to explore your thoughts, emotions, beliefs, and values related to gambling addiction. Cultivate mindfulness and present-moment awareness to observe your experiences without judgment or avoidance.
   - **External Feedback**: Seek feedback from trusted individuals, such as family members, friends, or counselors, to gain perspectives on how your gambling behavior impacts yourself and others. Listen openly to constructive feedback and integrate insights into your self-awareness journey.

2. **Benefits of Self-Awareness**:

- **Identifying Triggers**: Recognize personal triggers, cues, or situations that prompt gambling urges and cravings. By understanding the root causes of gambling behavior, you can implement proactive strategies to manage triggers effectively and prevent relapse.
- **Understanding Motivations**: Explore underlying motivations, needs, and desires that contribute to gambling addiction. Identify whether gambling serves as a coping mechanism for stress, a source of excitement or escape, or a means of seeking validation or social connection.
- **Recognizing Patterns**: Identify recurring patterns of behavior, thoughts, and emotions associated with gambling addiction. Become attuned to automatic responses, cognitive distortions, and emotional triggers that influence decision-making and risk-taking behaviors.
- **Promoting Emotional Regulation**: Develop skills for recognizing and regulating emotions, such as mindfulness practices, relaxation techniques, or cognitive-behavioral strategies. Enhance emotional intelligence to navigate challenging emotions without resorting to gambling as a coping mechanism.

3. **Strategies for Building Self-Awareness**:
   - **Journaling**: Keep a journal or diary to record thoughts, feelings, and experiences related to gambling addiction. Reflect on triggers, cravings, successes,

setbacks, and insights gained throughout your recovery journey.
   - **Self-Reflection Exercises**: Engage in structured self-reflection exercises, such as guided prompts or questions, to explore personal values, strengths, vulnerabilities, and growth areas. Consider how gambling addiction has impacted various domains of your life, including relationships, finances, and well-being.
   - **Mindfulness Practices**: Practice mindfulness meditation, deep breathing exercises, or body scans to cultivate present-moment awareness and nonjudgmental acceptance of thoughts and sensations. Mindfulness promotes clarity of mind, emotional regulation, and detachment from habitual patterns of behavior.
   - **Therapeutic Techniques**: Participate in therapy or counseling sessions focused on enhancing self-awareness, exploring underlying issues contributing to gambling addiction, and developing insight into cognitive and emotional processes. Therapeutic modalities, such as cognitive-behavioral therapy (CBT) or motivational interviewing, encourage self-exploration and personal growth.
   - **Feedback and Accountability**: Seek feedback from supportive individuals or peers in recovery to gain external perspectives on your behavior, progress, and challenges. Establish accountability partnerships or support networks to share experiences, exchange insights, and receive encouragement in maintaining self-awareness.

4. **Integration into Daily Practice**:
   - **Consistency**: Incorporate self-awareness practices into your daily routine to promote continuity and ongoing growth in recovery. Dedicate time for self-reflection, mindfulness exercises, or journaling to deepen understanding of your thoughts, emotions, and behaviors.
   - **Reflection and Adaptation**: Reflect on your self-awareness journey regularly, identifying areas of growth, challenges, and opportunities for adaptation. Adapt self-awareness strategies based on evolving needs, experiences, and feedback received in the recovery process.
   - **Personal Development**: Embrace self-awareness as a lifelong journey of personal development and self-discovery. Cultivate curiosity, openness, and self-compassion in exploring your inner world and fostering greater authenticity, resilience, and well-being.

Building self-awareness empowers individuals recovering from gambling addiction to deepen their understanding of personal triggers, motivations, and patterns of behavior. By fostering introspection, mindfulness, and emotional intelligence, individuals can develop insights, navigate challenges, and cultivate adaptive strategies for sustainable recovery and personal growth.

Cultivating Resilience

Resilience is a fundamental quality that enhances individuals' ability to navigate challenges, overcome setbacks, and sustain motivation in the recovery journey from gambling addiction. By cultivating resilience, individuals can build inner strength, adaptability, and perseverance to thrive amidst adversity and promote long-term well-being.

1. **Definition of Resilience**:
   - **Adaptability**: Embrace flexibility and adaptability in response to changing circumstances, setbacks, or unexpected challenges in recovery. View challenges as opportunities for growth, learning, and personal development.
   - **Perseverance**: Demonstrate persistence, determination, and grit in pursuing recovery goals and overcoming obstacles along the journey. Maintain a positive outlook, even in the face of setbacks or temporary setbacks.
   - **Resourcefulness**: Utilize internal and external resources, such as coping skills, support networks, and professional guidance, to navigate challenges effectively and overcome adversity in recovery.
   - **Self-Compassion**: Practice self-compassion by treating yourself with kindness, understanding, and acceptance during difficult times. Acknowledge your efforts, progress, and resilience in overcoming gambling addiction.

- **Optimism**: Cultivate optimism and a hopeful outlook for the future, believing in your ability to achieve recovery goals, overcome challenges, and create positive change in your life.

2. **Factors Influencing Resilience**:
   - **Supportive Relationships**: Foster strong social connections with family members, friends, peers in recovery, or support groups who provide encouragement, empathy, and practical assistance. Seek guidance, feedback, and emotional support during challenging times.
   - **Coping Skills**: Develop adaptive coping skills, such as problem-solving, emotion regulation, stress management, and mindfulness techniques. Strengthen resilience by practicing effective coping strategies to navigate triggers and setbacks in recovery.
   - **Positive Mindset**: Cultivate a positive mindset and optimism about your ability to overcome adversity, learn from experiences, and achieve personal growth in recovery from gambling addiction. Focus on strengths, successes, and opportunities for improvement.
   - **Self-Efficacy**: Build confidence in your capabilities, strengths, and capacity to manage challenges, achieve goals, and maintain recovery from gambling addiction. Develop a sense of empowerment and belief in your ability to create positive change.
   - **Adaptive Thinking**: Foster adaptive thinking patterns, such as cognitive flexibility, problem-solving skills, and reframing challenges as opportunities for learning and growth. Challenge negative or

self-defeating thoughts that undermine resilience and motivation.

3. **Strategies for Cultivating Resilience**:
   - **Strengthening Social Support**: Build and nurture supportive relationships with individuals who understand your journey in recovery from gambling addiction. Seek encouragement, empathy, and practical assistance from trusted friends, family members, or support groups.
   - **Developing Coping Skills**: Enhance your repertoire of coping skills, such as mindfulness meditation, relaxation techniques, assertiveness training, and conflict resolution. Practice adaptive coping strategies to manage stress, cravings, and triggers effectively.
   - **Setting Realistic Expectations**: Establish realistic expectations for yourself in recovery, acknowledging that setbacks and challenges are natural parts of the process. Embrace a growth mindset focused on continuous improvement, learning, and resilience-building.
   - **Mindfulness and Self-Reflection**: Cultivate mindfulness practices, such as meditation, deep breathing, or body scans, to promote present-moment awareness and emotional regulation. Engage in regular self-reflection to assess progress, identify strengths, and adapt resilience-building strategies.
   - **Seeking Professional Support**: Consult with therapists, counselors, or addiction specialists experienced in gambling addiction and resilience-building techniques. Participate in individual

therapy, group therapy, or educational workshops to gain insights, skills, and support in cultivating resilience.

4. **Integration into Daily Life**:
   - **Consistency**: Integrate resilience-building practices into your daily routine to foster continuity and habituation. Dedicate time for self-care, social connection, stress management, and personal reflection to sustain resilience and well-being.
   - **Adaptation and Flexibility**: Adapt resilience-building strategies based on evolving needs, experiences, and challenges encountered in recovery. Remain flexible in adjusting strategies, seeking new resources, and learning from setbacks to enhance resilience over time.
   - **Continuous Growth**: Embrace resilience as an ongoing process of personal growth, adaptation, and empowerment in recovery from gambling addiction. Cultivate resilience as a foundational strength that supports your journey toward long-term sobriety, well-being, and fulfillment.

   Cultivating resilience empowers individuals recovering from gambling addiction to navigate challenges.

Chapter 5: Seeking Professional Help

Types of Professional Treatment

Seeking professional help is a pivotal step in the journey to recovery from gambling addiction, offering individuals access to specialized care, evidence-based interventions, and comprehensive support systems tailored to their unique needs. This chapter explores various types of professional treatment options available to individuals grappling with gambling addiction, emphasizing the importance of seeking expert guidance to facilitate healing, promote behavior change, and foster long-term recovery.

1. **Individual Therapy**:
   - **Cognitive-Behavioral Therapy (CBT)**: CBT is a widely recognized and effective therapeutic approach for treating gambling addiction. It focuses on identifying and challenging distorted thoughts, beliefs, and behaviors associated with gambling, teaching coping skills, and promoting behavioral change. Through structured sessions, individuals learn to manage triggers, develop alternative coping strategies, and address underlying psychological factors contributing to gambling behavior.
   - **Motivational Interviewing (MI)**: MI is a client-centered therapeutic technique designed to explore ambivalence, enhance motivation for change, and strengthen commitment to recovery goals.

Therapists employ empathetic listening, reflective questioning, and collaborative goal-setting to elicit intrinsic motivation, resolve ambivalence, and empower individuals to initiate and sustain behavioral changes related to gambling addiction.

   - **Psychodynamic Therapy**: Psychodynamic therapy explores unconscious conflicts, early life experiences, and interpersonal dynamics that may underlie gambling addiction. Therapists help individuals gain insight into underlying emotions, motivations, and relational patterns influencing gambling behavior, facilitating emotional processing, self-discovery, and personal growth.

2. **Group Therapy**:
   - **Cognitive-Behavioral Group Therapy**: CBT group therapy incorporates cognitive-behavioral techniques within a supportive group setting. Participants share experiences, learn from peers, practice new skills, and receive feedback and encouragement in a structured environment. Group therapy fosters social connection, mutual support, and accountability among individuals recovering from gambling addiction, promoting empathy, shared learning, and collective problem-solving.
   - **Support Groups (e.g., Gamblers Anonymous)**: Support groups provide peer support, guidance, and solidarity to individuals affected by gambling addiction. Based on principles of mutual aid and shared experience, support groups offer a nonjudgmental space for individuals to discuss challenges, share coping strategies, and receive encouragement from others

facing similar struggles. Meetings may incorporate elements of fellowship, spiritual guidance, and personal accountability, empowering participants to maintain abstinence, navigate triggers, and foster personal growth in recovery.

3. **Family Therapy**:
   - **Family-Based Interventions**: Family therapy involves the participation of family members in the therapeutic process to address interpersonal dynamics, communication patterns, and family roles that may contribute to or be impacted by gambling addiction. Therapists help families improve understanding, empathy, and support for the individual in recovery, facilitate conflict resolution, and strengthen family relationships. Family therapy enhances familial involvement in the recovery journey, promotes collective healing, and reduces relapse risk by fostering a supportive and cohesive family environment.

4. **Specialized Treatment Programs**:
   - **Residential Treatment Centers**: Residential treatment centers offer intensive, structured programs for individuals with severe gambling addiction or co-occurring mental health disorders. Participants reside onsite for a designated period, receiving comprehensive therapeutic interventions, 24/7 medical and psychological support, and immersive recovery-oriented activities. Residential programs provide a therapeutic milieu conducive to healing, personal growth, and sustained recovery from gambling addiction.

- **Outpatient Programs**: Outpatient programs provide flexible, non-residential treatment options tailored to individuals' schedules, commitments, and treatment needs. Participants attend therapy sessions, group meetings, and educational workshops at specified intervals, receiving personalized support, skill-building strategies, and ongoing monitoring of progress in recovery. Outpatient programs facilitate continuity of care, promote community integration, and empower individuals to manage gambling addiction while maintaining daily responsibilities and routines.

Finding the Right Therapist or Counselor

Finding the right therapist or counselor is a crucial decision for individuals seeking professional help for gambling addiction, as the therapeutic relationship plays a pivotal role in treatment outcomes, recovery progress, and personal growth. This section explores considerations, guidelines, and strategies for selecting a qualified and compatible therapist or counselor who can provide effective support, guidance, and therapeutic interventions tailored to individual needs.

1. **Qualifications and Credentials**:
  - **Licensed Professionals**: Choose therapists or counselors who are licensed, accredited, and certified by reputable professional organizations, such as state licensing boards, national counseling associations, or addiction treatment agencies. Verify credentials, educational background, specialized training in

gambling addiction treatment, and adherence to ethical standards and professional guidelines.
   - **Specialization in Gambling Addiction**: Seek professionals with expertise, experience, and specialized training in treating gambling addiction and co-occurring mental health disorders. Specialized knowledge equips therapists to address the complexities of gambling behavior, implement evidence-based interventions, and support individuals in achieving sustained recovery and well-being.
   - **Continuing Education and Professional Development**: Inquire about therapists' ongoing education, training, and participation in professional development activities related to gambling addiction treatment. Commitment to staying abreast of current research, treatment modalities, and best practices ensures competent, informed, and effective therapeutic care.

2. **Therapeutic Approach and Compatibility**:
   - **Treatment Philosophy**: Discuss therapists' therapeutic approach, treatment philosophy, and methods used in addressing gambling addiction. Evaluate compatibility with personal preferences, goals for recovery, and comfort level with therapeutic techniques, such as cognitive-behavioral therapy, motivational interviewing, or psychodynamic therapy.
   - **Communication Style**: Assess therapists' communication style, interpersonal skills, and ability to establish a trusting, collaborative therapeutic relationship. Seek therapists who demonstrate empathy,

active listening, cultural sensitivity, and respect for individual differences in background, values, and experiences.
   - **Client-Centered Approach**: Prioritize therapists who adopt a client-centered approach to treatment, prioritizing your unique needs, preferences, and goals for recovery. Collaboration, shared decision-making, and mutual respect promote a therapeutic alliance characterized by trust, openness, and empowerment in addressing gambling addiction.

3. **Referrals and Recommendations**:
   - **Professional Referrals**: Seek referrals from healthcare providers, primary care physicians, or mental health professionals familiar with gambling addiction treatment. Consult trusted sources, such as addiction treatment centers, community resources, or support groups, for recommendations on qualified therapists or counselors specializing in gambling addiction.
   - **Peer Support**: Utilize peer support networks, such as support groups or online forums for individuals in recovery from gambling addiction, to gather recommendations, testimonials, and firsthand experiences with therapists or counselors. Peer insights provide valuable perspectives and guidance in selecting a therapist who aligns with your recovery needs and preferences.

4. **Initial Consultation and Assessment**:
   - **Exploratory Sessions**: Schedule initial consultations or exploratory sessions with potential

therapists or counselors to assess compatibility, establish rapport, and discuss treatment goals. Use this opportunity to ask questions about therapists' expertise, approach to gambling addiction treatment, anticipated outcomes, and collaborative treatment planning.

   - **Assessment of Fit**: Evaluate your comfort level, trust, and sense of connection with the therapist during the initial consultation. Consider factors such as therapeutic rapport, ease of communication, and alignment of treatment goals to determine whether the therapist's approach and style resonate with your preferences and expectations for therapy.

5. **Continuity of Care and Support**:
   - **Treatment Coordination**: Choose therapists or counselors who prioritize continuity of care, interdisciplinary collaboration, and comprehensive support throughout the recovery journey. Collaborate with therapists in developing personalized treatment plans, setting realistic goals, and integrating therapeutic interventions aligned with your evolving needs in gambling addiction treatment.
   - **Follow-up and Feedback**: Maintain open communication with therapists or counselors to provide feedback, address concerns, and monitor progress in therapy. Advocate for personalized care, ongoing evaluation of treatment effectiveness, and adjustments to therapeutic strategies to optimize recovery outcomes and promote long-term well-being.

   Finding the right therapist or counselor is a collaborative process that requires thoughtful consideration, informed decision-making, and alignment with your goals for recovery from gambling addiction. By prioritizing qualifications, therapeutic approach, compatibility, and continuity of care, individuals can cultivate a supportive therapeutic relationship, receive effective treatment, and embark on a transformative journey toward sustained recovery and personal growth.

The Role of Support Groups

Support groups play a vital role in the recovery journey from gambling addiction, offering individuals affected by gambling disorder a supportive community, shared understanding, and practical strategies for coping, healing, and maintaining abstinence. This section explores the significance of support groups, types of groups available, and benefits of peer support in promoting recovery, fostering resilience, and enhancing overall well-being.

1. **Types of Support Groups**:
   - **Gamblers Anonymous (GA)**: Gamblers Anonymous is a fellowship of individuals recovering from gambling addiction, following a 12-step program model adapted from Alcoholics Anonymous (AA). GA meetings provide a safe, confidential space for sharing experiences, discussing challenges, and receiving mutual support from peers committed to abstinence from gambling.
   - **SMART Recovery**: SMART Recovery offers science-based, self-empowering support groups for

individuals recovering from addictive behaviors, including gambling addiction. SMART Recovery emphasizes cognitive-behavioral techniques, motivational strategies, and skill-building exercises to promote sustainable behavior change, enhance coping skills, and foster personal growth.

   - **Online Support Groups**: Online support groups, forums, and virtual meetings provide accessible, convenient platforms for individuals to connect with peers, share experiences, and access resources related to gambling addiction recovery. Online support groups offer anonymity, flexibility, and global reach, facilitating peer support, information exchange, and social connection across diverse backgrounds and geographical locations.

2. **Benefits of Support Groups**:
   - **Peer Support**: Engage in peer support networks to connect with individuals who understand the challenges of gambling addiction, share similar experiences, and provide empathy, encouragement, and practical guidance in recovery. Peer support fosters a sense of belonging, reduces isolation, and promotes solidarity in

 navigating the complexities of addiction and recovery.
   - **Shared Experience**: Participate in support group meetings to listen to others' stories, perspectives, and strategies for overcoming gambling addiction. Gain insights into common triggers, coping mechanisms, and recovery milestones, learning from diverse experiences

and approaches to maintaining abstinence and promoting well-being.

   - **Accountability and Motivation**: Benefit from accountability partnerships, sponsorship, and peer encouragement in setting and achieving recovery goals. Support groups provide a structured framework for goal setting, progress monitoring, and celebrating achievements, reinforcing commitment to sobriety and personal growth.

   - **Skill Development**: Acquire practical skills, coping strategies, and resilience-building techniques through group discussions, educational materials, and experiential exercises offered in support group settings. Develop interpersonal skills, assertiveness, problem-solving abilities, and emotional regulation strategies essential for navigating triggers, managing cravings, and maintaining recovery from gambling addiction.

3. **Community and Connection**:

   - **Social Connection**: Cultivate meaningful relationships, friendships, and social connections within support groups that extend beyond addiction recovery. Participate in social activities, recreational events, and community initiatives organized by support groups to build social support networks, enhance well-being, and foster a sense of community among individuals committed to sobriety and personal growth.

   - **Peer Leadership and Mentorship**: Engage in peer leadership roles, mentorship opportunities, and service commitments within support groups to contribute positively to the recovery community, inspire hope, and support others on their journey toward sustained abstinence and holistic well-being.

Support groups serve as invaluable resources in the recovery journey from gambling addiction, offering peer support, shared understanding, and practical strategies for achieving and maintaining sobriety. By actively participating in support groups, individuals can cultivate resilience, enhance coping skills, and build a supportive network of peers committed to personal growth, recovery, and lifelong well-being.

Chapter 6: Self-Help Strategies

Self-help strategies are vital components of the recovery process for individuals grappling with gambling addiction. These strategies empower individuals to take control of their recovery, build resilience, and develop skills necessary for long-term abstinence and well-being. This chapter explores various self-help strategies, including developing healthy habits, mindfulness and meditation, journaling and reflection, and cognitive-behavioral techniques, offering detailed guidance and practical tools to support individuals on their journey to recovery.

Developing Healthy Habits

Developing healthy habits is foundational to recovery from gambling addiction. Establishing routines and practices that promote physical, mental, and emotional well-being helps individuals replace harmful behaviors with positive, life-affirming activities. This section delves into various healthy habits that support recovery and enhance overall quality of life.

1. **Physical Exercise**:
   - **Benefits of Exercise**: Regular physical activity reduces stress, anxiety, and depression, all of which can trigger gambling behavior. Exercise releases endorphins, the body's natural mood lifters, promoting a sense of well-being and enhancing mental health.

How to stop gambling by Lucky Willis

- **Types of Exercise**: Engage in a variety of physical activities, such as walking, running, swimming, cycling, yoga, and strength training. Experiment with different forms of exercise to find activities that you enjoy and can sustain long-term.
- **Creating a Routine**: Establish a consistent exercise routine by scheduling workouts at the same time each day or week. Set realistic goals and gradually increase the intensity and duration of your workouts to build stamina and avoid burnout.

2. **Balanced Nutrition**:
   - **Nutritional Needs**: Consuming a balanced diet rich in essential nutrients supports brain health, energy levels, and emotional stability. Nutritional deficiencies can exacerbate mood swings, cravings, and stress, all of which can contribute to gambling behavior.
   - **Healthy Eating Habits**: Incorporate a variety of whole foods, including fruits, vegetables, lean proteins, whole grains, and healthy fats, into your diet. Avoid processed foods, excessive sugar, and caffeine, which can negatively impact mood and energy levels.
   - **Meal Planning**: Plan meals and snacks in advance to ensure you have healthy options readily available. Preparing meals at home allows you to control ingredients and portion sizes, promoting better nutritional choices and reducing the temptation to gamble out of convenience or stress.

3. **Sleep Hygiene**:

- **Importance of Sleep**: Quality sleep is essential for emotional regulation, cognitive function, and overall well-being. Sleep deprivation can increase vulnerability to stress, anxiety, and impulsive behavior, all of which can trigger gambling urges.
- **Establishing a Routine**: Create a consistent sleep schedule by going to bed and waking up at the same time each day. Develop a relaxing bedtime routine, such as reading, taking a warm bath, or practicing relaxation techniques, to signal your body that it's time to sleep.
- **Sleep Environment**: Optimize your sleep environment by keeping your bedroom cool, dark, and quiet. Invest in a comfortable mattress and pillows, and minimize exposure to screens and bright lights before bedtime.

4. **Stress Management**:
    - **Identifying Stressors**: Recognize and identify sources of stress in your life, whether they are related to work, relationships, finances, or other areas. Understanding your stressors allows you to develop targeted strategies to manage them effectively.
    - **Relaxation Techniques**: Practice relaxation techniques such as deep breathing exercises, progressive muscle relaxation, and visualization to reduce stress and promote a sense of calm. Regular relaxation practices can help you manage stress in the moment and build resilience over time.
    - **Time Management**: Develop effective time management skills to balance responsibilities, reduce overwhelm, and create time for self-care activities.

Prioritize tasks, set realistic goals, and use tools such as calendars, planners, and to-do lists to stay organized and focused.

5. **Social Connections**:
   - **Building Support Networks**: Surround yourself with supportive and positive people who encourage your recovery journey. Building strong social connections provides emotional support, accountability, and a sense of belonging.
   - **Participating in Activities**: Engage in social activities that do not involve gambling, such as joining clubs, attending community events, or participating in recreational sports. Socializing in non-gambling environments helps you build healthy relationships and enjoy life without the need to gamble.
   - **Communicating Openly**: Practice open and honest communication with friends, family, and support group members about your struggles, progress, and needs in recovery. Sharing your experiences fosters understanding, reduces isolation, and strengthens your support network.

   Developing healthy habits is a proactive and empowering approach to recovery from gambling addiction. By incorporating physical exercise, balanced nutrition, quality sleep, stress management, and social connections into your daily routine, you create a solid foundation for long-term well-being and resilience in the face of challenges.

Mindfulness and Meditation

Mindfulness and meditation are powerful tools that enhance self-awareness, emotional regulation, and overall well-being. These practices help individuals cultivate a non-judgmental awareness of the present moment, allowing them to manage cravings, reduce stress, and develop healthier responses to triggers. This section explores various mindfulness and meditation techniques and their application in the context of gambling addiction recovery.

1. **Mindfulness Practice**:
   - **Definition and Principles**: Mindfulness involves paying attention to the present moment with openness, curiosity, and acceptance. It encourages individuals to observe their thoughts, feelings, and bodily sensations without judgment, fostering a deeper understanding of their inner experiences.
   - **Breath Awareness**: Practice focusing on your breath as an anchor to the present moment. Notice the sensation of the breath entering and leaving your body, and gently bring your attention back to the breath whenever your mind wanders.
   - **Body Scan Meditation**: Engage in a body scan meditation by directing your attention to different parts of your body, from head to toe. Notice any sensations, tension, or discomfort, and practice releasing any tension with each exhale. This practice promotes relaxation and a sense of connection to your body.

2. **Meditation Techniques**:
   - **Guided Meditation**: Use guided meditation recordings or apps to follow along with a meditation practice led by a teacher or narrator. Guided meditations can help you stay focused and provide structured support for developing your meditation practice.
   - **Loving-Kindness Meditation**: Practice loving-kindness meditation by silently repeating phrases that express goodwill, compassion, and kindness toward yourself and others. Begin with phrases such as "May I be happy, may I be healthy, may I be safe, may I live with ease," and gradually extend these wishes to others, including loved ones and even those with whom you have conflicts.
   - **Mindful Movement**: Incorporate mindful movement practices, such as yoga, tai chi, or qigong, into your routine. These practices combine physical movement with mindful awareness, promoting relaxation, balance, and a deeper connection between mind and body.

3. **Application in Recovery**:
   - **Managing Cravings**: Use mindfulness techniques to observe and sit with cravings without reacting to them. Notice the sensations, thoughts, and emotions associated with cravings, and practice allowing them to pass without engaging in gambling behavior.
   - **Reducing Stress**: Practice mindfulness and meditation to reduce stress and enhance emotional regulation. By cultivating a sense of calm and

centeredness, you can respond to stressors more effectively and reduce the likelihood of turning to gambling as a coping mechanism.

   - **Enhancing Self-Awareness**: Mindfulness and meditation help you become more aware of your thoughts, feelings, and behaviors, allowing you to identify patterns, triggers, and underlying emotions related to gambling addiction. Increased self-awareness supports informed decision-making and empowers you to make positive changes in your recovery journey.

   Mindfulness and meditation are transformative practices that promote self-awareness, emotional regulation, and overall well-being. By incorporating these techniques into your daily routine, you can enhance your ability to manage cravings, reduce stress, and cultivate a deeper connection to yourself and the present moment.

Journaling and Reflection

   Journaling and reflection are powerful self-help strategies that facilitate self-discovery, emotional processing, and personal growth. By regularly writing about your thoughts, feelings, and experiences, you can gain insights into your behaviors, track your progress, and develop a deeper understanding of your recovery journey. This section explores various journaling techniques and their benefits in the context of gambling addiction recovery.

1. **Types of Journaling**:

How to stop gambling by Lucky Willis

   - **Daily Journaling**: Establish a daily journaling practice to reflect on your thoughts, emotions, and experiences. Write about your day, any challenges you faced, and how you responded to them. Daily journaling helps you develop a habit of self-reflection and provides a record of your progress over time.
   - **Gratitude Journaling**: Focus on writing about things you are grateful for each day. Gratitude journaling shifts your attention to positive aspects of your life, enhancing your mood and fostering a sense of appreciation and contentment. Reflecting on gratitude can counteract negative thoughts and reduce the urge to gamble as a means of escaping negative emotions.
   - **Trigger Journaling**: Use your journal to identify and explore triggers that lead to gambling urges. Write about specific situations, thoughts, or emotions that trigger the desire to gamble, and reflect on how you can manage or avoid these triggers in the future. Understanding your triggers empowers you to develop effective coping strategies.

2. **Reflective Writing**:
   - **Exploring Emotions**: Write about your emotions in detail, describing how they feel in your body, what thoughts accompany them, and any underlying causes. Reflecting on your emotions helps you process and release them, reducing the likelihood of turning to gambling to cope with difficult feelings.
   - **Identifying Patterns**: Analyze your journaling entries to identify patterns in your thoughts, behaviors,

and emotions related to gambling. Recognize recurring themes, triggers, and coping mechanisms, and reflect on how you can address these patterns to support your recovery.

   - **Setting Goals**: Use your journal to set recovery goals and track your progress. Write about your short-term and long-term goals, the steps you need to take to achieve them, and any obstacles you anticipate. Regularly reviewing and updating your goals helps you stay motivated and focused on your recovery journey.

3. **Journaling Prompts**:
   - **Self-Reflection**: Use prompts such as "What am I feeling right now?", "What thoughts are going through my mind?", and "What do I need in this moment?" to guide your self-reflection. These prompts help you tune into your inner experiences and gain clarity about your needs and emotions.
   - **Progress and Growth**: Reflect on your progress by answering prompts like "What positive changes have I noticed in my life since starting my recovery?", "What challenges have I overcome?", and "What am I proud of today?" Celebrating your progress boosts your confidence and reinforces your commitment to recovery.
   - **Future Vision**: Envision your future by writing about "What does a gambling-free life look like for me?", "What are my hopes and dreams for the future?", and "How can I continue to grow and thrive in my recovery?"

Future-oriented journaling inspires hope and motivates you to stay on track with your recovery goals.

Journaling and reflection are valuable self-help strategies that support self-discovery, emotional processing, and personal growth. By regularly writing about your thoughts, feelings, and experiences, you can gain insights into your behaviors, track your progress, and develop a deeper understanding of your recovery journey.

Cognitive Behavioral Techniques

Cognitive-behavioral techniques (CBT) are evidence-based strategies that help individuals identify and change unhelpful thought patterns and behaviors associated with gambling addiction. CBT focuses on the interplay between thoughts, emotions, and behaviors, empowering individuals to develop healthier coping mechanisms and achieve long-term recovery. This section explores various cognitive-behavioral techniques and their application in the context of gambling addiction recovery.

1. **Identifying Cognitive Distortions**:
   - **Common Distortions**: Learn to recognize common cognitive distortions, such as all-or-nothing thinking, overgeneralization, catastrophizing, and personalization. These distorted thinking patterns can contribute to

negative emotions and impulsive behaviors, including gambling.

   - **Challenging Distortions**: Practice challenging cognitive distortions by examining the evidence for and against your thoughts, considering alternative perspectives, and identifying more balanced and realistic ways of thinking. For example, if you catch yourself thinking, "I'll never be able to stop gambling," challenge this thought by recalling past successes and considering the progress you've made in your recovery.

2. **Cognitive Restructuring**:
   - **Thought Records**: Use thought records to document and analyze your thoughts, emotions, and behaviors in response to specific situations. Identify triggering events, the automatic thoughts they elicit, the emotions and physical sensations that follow, and the resulting behaviors. Challenge and reframe unhelpful thoughts to develop more adaptive responses.
   - **Behavioral Experiments**: Conduct behavioral experiments to test the validity of your thoughts and beliefs. For example, if you believe that gambling is the only way to relieve stress, experiment with alternative stress-relief activities, such as exercise or mindfulness, and observe their effects. Behavioral experiments provide evidence to support more adaptive beliefs and behaviors.

3. **Developing Coping Strategies**:
   - **Problem-Solving Skills**: Enhance your problem-solving skills by systematically identifying

problems, generating potential solutions, evaluating the pros and cons of each option, and implementing and reviewing the chosen solution. Effective problem-solving reduces the likelihood of turning to gambling as a way to escape or cope with difficulties.
   - **Stress Management**: Develop a toolkit of stress management techniques, such as deep breathing exercises, progressive muscle relaxation, visualization, and mindfulness. Regularly practicing these techniques helps you manage stress more effectively and reduces the urge to gamble as a way to cope with stress.
   - **Relapse Prevention**: Create a relapse prevention plan that identifies potential high-risk situations, coping strategies, and support resources. Develop specific action plans for managing cravings, avoiding triggers, and seeking support when needed. A well-prepared relapse prevention plan enhances your ability to maintain abstinence and navigate challenges in recovery.

4. **Enhancing Self-Efficacy**:
   - **Building Confidence**: Practice activities that build your confidence and self-efficacy, such as setting and achieving small, manageable goals, seeking feedback and support from others, and reflecting on past successes. Developing a sense of self-efficacy enhances your belief in your ability to overcome challenges and achieve recovery.
   - **Positive Self-Talk**: Replace negative self-talk with positive, affirming statements that reinforce your strengths, capabilities, and progress. Practice

affirmations such as "I am strong and capable of overcoming this addiction," "I have the power to make positive changes," and "I am committed to my recovery and well-being."

- **Self-Compassion**: Cultivate self-compassion by treating yourself with kindness, understanding, and patience, especially during setbacks or challenges. Recognize that recovery is a journey with ups and downs, and practice self-compassionate responses to mistakes or lapses. Self-compassion fosters resilience and a more balanced perspective on your recovery journey.

Cognitive-behavioral techniques are powerful tools for identifying and changing unhelpful thought patterns and behaviors associated with gambling addiction. By incorporating these techniques into your recovery plan, you can develop healthier coping mechanisms, enhance self-efficacy, and achieve long-term well-being and sobriety.

Chapter 6 provides a comprehensive exploration of self-help strategies, including developing healthy habits, mindfulness and meditation, journaling and reflection, and cognitive-behavioral techniques. By integrating these strategies into your recovery journey, you can take control of your healing process, build resilience, and develop the skills necessary for long-term abstinence and well-being.

Chapter 7: Building a Support Network

Building a robust support network is a cornerstone of recovering from gambling addiction. A strong support network provides emotional, psychological, and practical support, offering encouragement, accountability, and a sense of community. This chapter explores the role of family and friends, joining support groups, utilizing online communities and resources, and maintaining supportive relationships to aid in the recovery journey.

The Role of Family and Friends

Family and friends play a crucial role in the recovery process, offering emotional support, understanding, and practical assistance. Their involvement can significantly impact the success of recovery efforts, providing a foundation of love and encouragement.

1. **Emotional Support**:
   - **Listening and Empathy**: Family and friends can offer a listening ear and empathize with the struggles and emotions associated with gambling addiction. Active listening, without judgment or criticism, allows the individual to feel heard and understood, which can be incredibly validating and comforting.

- **Encouragement and Motivation**: Encouragement from loved ones can bolster an individual's motivation to stay on track with recovery. Positive reinforcement and expressions of belief in the person's ability to overcome addiction can strengthen their resolve and commitment to change.
   - **Emotional Stability**: The presence of supportive family and friends provides emotional stability during difficult times. Knowing that there are people who care and are there to support can help mitigate feelings of isolation, anxiety, and depression that often accompany addiction.

2. **Practical Assistance**:
   - **Helping with Daily Tasks**: Family members and friends can assist with daily responsibilities, such as household chores, childcare, and financial management, to reduce stress and allow the individual to focus on recovery.
   - **Attending Appointments**: Accompanying the individual to therapy sessions, support group meetings, or medical appointments can provide moral support and help them stay committed to their recovery plan.
   - **Creating a Safe Environment**: Loved ones can help create a gambling-free environment by removing triggers and temptations, such as gambling paraphernalia, and by engaging in activities that do not involve gambling.

3. **Setting Boundaries**:

- **Establishing Healthy Boundaries**: Family and friends must set healthy boundaries to protect their well-being while supporting the individual in recovery. This may involve setting limits on financial assistance, not enabling gambling behavior, and maintaining their own self-care routines.
- **Communicating Expectations**: Open and honest communication about expectations and boundaries is essential. Discussing what behaviors are acceptable and what consequences will follow if boundaries are crossed helps create a clear and supportive framework for recovery.
- **Encouraging Responsibility**: Encouraging the individual to take responsibility for their actions and recovery process is crucial. While support is essential, it is also important for the person to develop self-efficacy and accountability in their journey to recovery.

4. **Family Therapy**:
    - **Benefits of Family Therapy**: Family therapy can help address underlying issues within the family system that may contribute to or be affected by the individual's gambling addiction. It provides a safe space for open communication, conflict resolution, and healing.
    - **Rebuilding Trust**: Gambling addiction can erode trust within relationships. Family therapy helps rebuild trust by facilitating honest dialogue, understanding each other's perspectives, and working together towards common goals.
    - **Strengthening Relationships**: Therapy can strengthen family relationships by improving

communication, fostering empathy, and developing healthier ways of interacting and supporting one another.

Family and friends play a multifaceted role in supporting recovery from gambling addiction. Their emotional and practical support, along with setting healthy boundaries and engaging in family therapy, can significantly enhance the individual's journey to recovery and well-being.

Joining Support Groups

Support groups provide a vital resource for individuals recovering from gambling addiction, offering peer support, shared experiences, and practical strategies for maintaining sobriety. Joining support groups can create a sense of community and provide essential encouragement and accountability.

1. **Types of Support Groups**:
   - **Peer-Led Groups**: Peer-led groups, such as Gamblers Anonymous (GA), are composed of individuals who share similar experiences with gambling addiction. These groups operate on a principle of mutual support, where members share their stories, offer advice, and provide encouragement to one another.
   - **Professionally-Led Groups**: Professionally-led support groups are facilitated by trained therapists or counselors who provide structure, guidance, and therapeutic interventions. These groups often focus on specific aspects of recovery, such as

cognitive-behavioral techniques, relapse prevention, or emotional regulation.
   - **Hybrid Groups**: Some support groups combine elements of both peer-led and professionally-led formats, offering the benefits of peer support along with professional oversight and therapeutic input.

2. **Benefits of Support Groups**:
   - **Shared Experiences**: Support groups provide a platform for individuals to share their experiences, challenges, and successes with others who understand what they are going through. This shared understanding fosters a sense of camaraderie and reduces feelings of isolation.
   - **Accountability**: Regular attendance at support group meetings helps individuals stay accountable to their recovery goals. Knowing that they will be sharing their progress with the group can motivate individuals to stay committed to their recovery plan.
   - **Practical Strategies**: Support group members often share practical strategies and coping mechanisms that have worked for them. This exchange of ideas and techniques can provide valuable insights and tools for managing triggers and maintaining sobriety.
   - **Emotional Support**: The emotional support provided by support group members can be invaluable, especially during challenging times. Members offer empathy, encouragement, and understanding, creating a supportive and nurturing environment.

3. **Finding and Joining a Support Group**:

- **Research and Resources**: Research local support groups, online directories, and resources provided by addiction treatment centers or mental health organizations. Websites like Gamblers Anonymous and the National Council on Problem Gambling offer information on support groups and meetings.
  - **Attending Meetings**: Attend several different support group meetings to find one that feels like a good fit. Each group has its own culture, dynamics, and focus, so it is important to find one where you feel comfortable and supported.
  - **Participation**: Actively participate in support group meetings by sharing your experiences, listening to others, and engaging in group activities. Participation helps build connections, foster trust, and enhance the benefits of the support group experience.

4. **Long-Term Engagement**:
   - **Regular Attendance**: Commit to regular attendance at support group meetings to maintain a consistent source of support and accountability. Regular engagement helps reinforce recovery principles and provides ongoing encouragement.
   - **Building Relationships**: Develop meaningful relationships with other support group members by connecting outside of meetings, attending social events, and participating in group activities. Building relationships enhances the sense of community and provides additional layers of support.
   - **Taking on Roles**: Consider taking on roles within the support group, such as facilitating meetings,

organizing events, or serving as a mentor to new members. Taking on roles increases your investment in the group and provides opportunities for personal growth and leadership.

Joining support groups offers a wealth of benefits for individuals recovering from gambling addiction, including shared experiences, accountability, practical strategies, and emotional support. Finding the right group and actively participating can significantly enhance the recovery journey and provide a strong foundation for long-term sobriety and well-being.

Online Communities and Resources

Online communities and resources provide convenient and accessible support for individuals recovering from gambling addiction. These platforms offer opportunities for connection, information, and support, regardless of geographical location or time constraints.

1. **Benefits of Online Communities**:
   - **Accessibility**: Online communities are accessible 24/7, allowing individuals to seek support and connect with others at any time. This accessibility is particularly beneficial for those who may not have access to local support groups or prefer the anonymity of online interactions.
   - **Diverse Perspectives**: Online communities often attract a diverse group of individuals from various backgrounds and experiences. This diversity provides a

wealth of perspectives, insights, and strategies for managing gambling addiction.
   - **Anonymity**: Online platforms offer a level of anonymity that can be comforting for individuals who may feel hesitant to share their struggles in person. Anonymity allows individuals to express themselves openly and honestly without fear of judgment.

2. **Types of Online Communities**:
   - **Forums and Discussion Boards**: Online forums and discussion boards, such as Reddit's "r/problemgambling" or dedicated gambling addiction forums, provide a space for individuals to share their experiences, ask questions, and offer support. These platforms facilitate ongoing conversations and peer support.
   - **Social Media Groups**: Social media platforms, such as Facebook, host various support groups dedicated to gambling addiction recovery. These groups provide a sense of community, opportunities for engagement, and access to resources and information.
   - **Online Meetings**: Many traditional support groups, such as Gamblers Anonymous, offer online meetings and virtual support groups. These meetings follow the same format as in-person meetings and provide the same benefits of shared experiences, accountability, and emotional support.

3. **Utilizing Online Resources**:
   - **Educational Materials**: Access educational materials, articles, and videos on reputable websites

dedicated to gambling addiction recovery. Websites such as the National Council on Problem Gambling and Gambling Therapy offer a wealth of information on the nature of addiction, treatment options, and coping strategies.
  - **Self-Help Tools**: Utilize self-help tools and resources available online, such as worksheets, self-assessment quizzes, and recovery apps. These tools can help individuals track their progress, identify triggers, and develop personalized recovery plans.
  - **Professional Support**: Many mental health professionals and addiction specialists offer online counseling and therapy services. Teletherapy provides convenient access to professional support and can be an effective component of a comprehensive recovery plan.

4. **Staying Safe Online**:
  - **Privacy and Security**: Protect your privacy and personal information when participating in online communities. Use anonymous usernames, avoid sharing identifiable information, and be cautious about clicking on links or downloading files

 from unknown sources.
  - **Setting Boundaries**: Set boundaries for your online interactions to prevent overreliance on digital support and ensure a balanced approach to recovery. Limit the time spent online, and prioritize in-person connections and activities that promote well-being.

- **Evaluating Resources**: Evaluate the credibility and reliability of online resources and communities. Look for reputable websites, verified professionals, and well-moderated groups to ensure you receive accurate and trustworthy information and support.

Online communities and resources offer valuable support for individuals recovering from gambling addiction, providing accessibility, diverse perspectives, and anonymity. By actively engaging with online platforms and utilizing available resources, individuals can enhance their recovery journey and build a strong foundation for long-term sobriety.

Maintaining Supportive Relationships

Maintaining supportive relationships is essential for sustaining recovery from gambling addiction. Positive and healthy relationships provide ongoing encouragement, accountability, and a sense of connection, which are crucial for long-term well-being and sobriety.

1. **Nurturing Existing Relationships**:
   - **Open Communication**: Foster open and honest communication with family and friends about your recovery journey. Share your experiences, challenges, and successes, and encourage them to do the same. Transparent communication builds trust and mutual understanding.

- **Expressing Gratitude**: Show appreciation and gratitude to those who support you in your recovery. Acknowledge their efforts, express your thanks, and let them know how much their support means to you. Gratitude strengthens relationships and fosters a positive and supportive environment.
   - **Spending Quality Time**: Invest time in nurturing relationships by engaging in activities that you enjoy together. Spending quality time with loved ones strengthens bonds and creates positive experiences that support your well-being.

2. **Setting Healthy Boundaries**:
   - **Defining Boundaries**: Clearly define and communicate your boundaries to family and friends. Explain what behaviors are acceptable and what you need from them to support your recovery. Setting boundaries helps protect your well-being and ensures that relationships remain healthy and supportive.
   - **Respecting Boundaries**: Respect the boundaries set by others and be mindful of their needs and limitations. Mutual respect and understanding create a balanced and harmonious dynamic in relationships.
   - **Managing Conflict**: Address conflicts and disagreements in a constructive and respectful manner. Use active listening, empathy, and problem-solving skills to resolve issues and maintain healthy relationships.

3. **Building New Supportive Relationships**:
   - **Expanding Your Network**: Seek out opportunities to build new supportive relationships by joining clubs,

organizations, or community groups that align with your interests and values. Expanding your social network provides additional sources of support and connection.
   - **Finding Mentors**: Identify mentors or role models who can offer guidance, support, and inspiration in your recovery journey. Mentors can provide valuable insights, share their experiences, and offer encouragement and advice.
   - **Engaging in Social Activities**: Participate in social activities and events that promote positive interactions and foster new connections. Engaging in social activities helps build a sense of community and belonging.

4. **Maintaining Accountability**:
   - **Regular Check-Ins**: Schedule regular check-ins with trusted family members, friends, or support group members to discuss your progress, challenges, and goals. Regular check-ins provide accountability and ongoing support.
   - **Accountability Partners**: Establish accountability partnerships with individuals who are committed to supporting your recovery. Accountability partners can help you stay on track with your goals, provide encouragement, and offer a listening ear when needed.
   - **Monitoring Progress**: Keep track of your progress and share updates with your support network. Monitoring your progress and receiving feedback from others reinforces your commitment to recovery and provides motivation to continue making positive changes.

5. **Developing Healthy Relationship Skills**:
   - **Effective Communication**: Practice effective communication skills, such as active listening, assertiveness, and empathy, to enhance your interactions with others. Effective communication fosters understanding and connection.
   - **Emotional Regulation**: Develop emotional regulation skills to manage your emotions and respond to situations in a healthy and constructive manner. Techniques such as deep breathing, mindfulness, and cognitive restructuring can help you regulate your emotions.
   - **Conflict Resolution**: Learn and practice conflict resolution skills to address and resolve disagreements in a healthy and respectful way. Effective conflict resolution involves active listening, empathy, problem-solving, and compromise.

Maintaining supportive relationships is a key component of sustaining recovery from gambling addiction. By nurturing existing relationships, setting healthy boundaries, building new connections, maintaining accountability, and developing healthy relationship skills, individuals can create a strong support network that promotes long-term well-being and sobriety.

Chapter 7 provides a comprehensive exploration of building a support network, including the role of family and friends, joining support groups, utilizing online communities and resources, and maintaining supportive relationships. By actively engaging in these areas, individuals can strengthen their recovery journey and

How to stop gambling by Lucky Willis

build a solid foundation for long-term sobriety and well-being.

Chapter 8: Financial Recovery and Management

Recovering from gambling addiction involves not only addressing the psychological and emotional aspects but also dealing with the financial repercussions. Financial recovery and management are crucial for rebuilding stability and achieving long-term sobriety. This chapter delves into assessing your financial situation, creating a financial plan, avoiding financial triggers, and seeking financial counseling.

Assessing Your Financial Situation

The first step in financial recovery is to gain a clear understanding of your current financial situation. This involves taking a thorough inventory of your assets, liabilities, income, and expenses.

1. **Gathering Financial Information**:
   - **Documenting Assets and Liabilities**: List all your assets, including bank accounts, investments, property, and any other valuable possessions. Then, list all your liabilities, such as credit card debt, loans, and unpaid bills. This will give you a comprehensive view of your net worth.

How to stop gambling by Lucky Willis

- **Tracking Income and Expenses**: Document your sources of income, including salary, bonuses, freelance work, and any other earnings. Track your expenses, including fixed costs (rent, utilities, loan payments) and variable costs (groceries, entertainment, discretionary spending). Use financial tracking tools or spreadsheets to organize this information.

2. **Analyzing Spending Patterns**:
   - **Identifying Problematic Spending**: Review your spending habits to identify areas where gambling has caused financial strain. Look for patterns such as frequent cash withdrawals, payments to gambling establishments, or excessive discretionary spending. Understanding these patterns can help you recognize where changes are needed.
   - **Calculating the Impact of Gambling**: Calculate the total amount spent on gambling over a specific period. This will give you a clear picture of the financial impact of your gambling behavior and serve as a motivator for change.

3. **Setting Financial Goals**:
   - **Short-Term Goals**: Establish short-term financial goals, such as creating a budget, paying off a specific debt, or saving a certain amount each month.
   Short-term goals should be achievable and provide a sense of immediate progress.
   - **Long-Term Goals**: Set long-term financial goals, such as building an emergency fund, saving for a major purchase, or planning for retirement. Long-term goals

require a sustained effort and help create a vision for a financially stable future.

4. **Assessing Credit and Debt**:
   - **Obtaining Credit Reports**: Obtain copies of your credit reports from major credit reporting agencies. Review them for accuracy and identify any areas of concern, such as overdue accounts or high credit card balances.
   - **Evaluating Debt Repayment**: Assess your ability to repay outstanding debts. Prioritize high-interest debts and consider options such as debt consolidation, negotiating with creditors, or setting up a repayment plan.

5. **Creating a Financial Snapshot**:
   - **Net Worth Statement**: Create a net worth statement by subtracting your total liabilities from your total assets. This provides a snapshot of your overall financial health and can be updated regularly to track your progress.
   - **Cash Flow Statement**: Develop a cash flow statement that tracks your monthly income and expenses. This helps you understand where your money is going and identify areas for improvement.

   Assessing your financial situation provides a solid foundation for creating a realistic and effective financial recovery plan. By gathering financial information, analyzing spending patterns, setting goals, and assessing credit and debt, you can take control of your financial health and work towards stability and recovery.

Creating a Financial Plan

Once you have a clear understanding of your financial situation, the next step is to create a comprehensive financial plan. A financial plan outlines your income, expenses, savings, and debt repayment strategies, helping you manage your money effectively and achieve your financial goals.

1. **Developing a Budget**:
   - **Income Allocation**: Allocate your income to cover essential expenses, such as housing, utilities, groceries, transportation, and healthcare. Ensure that your basic needs are met before allocating money to discretionary spending.
   - **Discretionary Spending**: Limit discretionary spending by setting aside a specific amount for non-essential items, such as dining out, entertainment, and hobbies. Track this spending closely to avoid overspending.
   - **Savings Goals**: Allocate a portion of your income to savings goals, such as building an emergency fund, saving for a major purchase, or contributing to retirement accounts. Aim to save a percentage of your income each month, even if it is a small amount.

2. **Debt Repayment Strategies**:
   - **Prioritizing Debts**: Prioritize debts based on interest rates and urgency. Focus on paying off

high-interest debts first, as they accrue more interest over time and can become more burdensome.

   - **Debt Snowball Method**: Consider using the debt snowball method, where you pay off the smallest debts first to build momentum and motivation. Once a small debt is paid off, move on to the next smallest debt, gradually eliminating all debts.

   - **Debt Avalanche Method**: Alternatively, use the debt avalanche method, where you focus on paying off debts with the highest interest rates first. This method can save you more money in interest payments over time.

3. **Building an Emergency Fund**:

   - **Importance of an Emergency Fund**: An emergency fund provides financial security in case of unexpected expenses, such as medical bills, car repairs, or job loss. Aim to save three to six months' worth of living expenses in a separate, easily accessible account.

   - **Automating Savings**: Automate your savings by setting up automatic transfers from your checking account to your emergency fund. This ensures consistent contributions and reduces the temptation to spend the money elsewhere.

4. **Long-Term Financial Planning**:

   - **Retirement Planning**: Start planning for retirement by contributing to retirement accounts, such as 401(k)s or IRAs. Take advantage of employer matching contributions if available and consider increasing your contributions over time.

- **Investment Strategies**: Explore investment options to grow your wealth over the long term. Consider consulting with a financial advisor to develop a diversified investment portfolio that aligns with your risk tolerance and financial goals.
- **Estate Planning**: Develop an estate plan to ensure that your assets are distributed according to your wishes. This may include creating a will, setting up trusts, and designating beneficiaries for retirement accounts and life insurance policies.

5. **Monitoring and Adjusting Your Plan**:
   - **Regular Review**: Regularly review your financial plan to track your progress and make adjustments as needed. Update your budget, debt repayment strategies, and savings goals to reflect changes in your financial situation.
   - **Adapting to Changes**: Be prepared to adapt your financial plan in response to life changes, such as a new job, marriage, the birth of a child, or unexpected expenses. Flexibility is key to maintaining financial stability and achieving your goals.

Creating a financial plan provides a structured approach to managing your money, reducing debt, and building savings. By developing a budget, prioritizing debt repayment, building an emergency fund, planning for the long term, and regularly reviewing your plan, you can achieve financial recovery and stability.

Avoiding Financial Triggers

Avoiding financial triggers is crucial for maintaining recovery from gambling addiction. Financial triggers can lead to impulsive decisions and relapse, undermining your progress and financial stability. This section explores strategies for identifying and managing financial triggers.

1. **Identifying Financial Triggers**:
   - **Emotional Triggers**: Recognize emotional triggers that lead to gambling, such as stress, boredom, loneliness, or excitement. Understanding these emotions can help you develop healthier coping mechanisms.
   - **Situational Triggers**: Identify situational triggers, such as visiting places associated with gambling, being around people who gamble, or having access to large amounts of cash. Avoiding these situations can reduce the temptation to gamble.
   - **Financial Triggers**: Acknowledge financial triggers, such as receiving a large sum of money, having easy access to credit, or experiencing financial stress. Managing your finances effectively can help mitigate these triggers.

2. **Developing Healthy Financial Habits**:
   - **Budgeting and Planning**: Stick to a budget and plan your spending to avoid impulsive financial decisions. Use budgeting apps or tools to track your expenses and stay on top of your financial goals.

How to stop gambling by Lucky Willis

- **Cash Management**: Limit the amount of cash you carry to reduce the temptation to gamble. Use debit or credit cards for necessary purchases and keep cash reserves in a secure location.
- **Financial Accountability**: Establish financial accountability by sharing your financial goals and progress with a trusted friend or family member. Regularly discuss your financial situation and seek their support in staying on track.

3. **Managing Access to Money**:
   - **Restricting Access**: Consider restricting access to large sums of money or credit by setting up safeguards. This may include placing limits on your credit cards, setting up direct deposits to a trusted person, or using prepaid cards for daily expenses.
   - **Joint Accounts**: Use joint accounts with a trusted family member or friend to monitor spending and ensure accountability. This can help you stay disciplined and avoid impulsive financial decisions.
   - **Financial Controls**: Implement financial controls, such as automatic bill payments and savings transfers, to reduce the need for manual financial management and minimize opportunities for impulsive spending.

4. **Replacing Gambling with Positive Activities**:
   - **Hobbies and Interests**: Engage in hobbies and activities that bring you joy and fulfillment. Finding alternative ways to spend your time can help reduce the urge to gamble.

- **Social Connections**: Strengthen social connections by spending time with family and friends, joining clubs or groups, and participating in community activities. Positive social interactions provide support and reduce feelings of isolation.
- **Physical Activity**: Incorporate physical activity into your routine, such as walking, running, yoga, or team sports. Exercise can reduce stress, improve mood, and provide a healthy outlet for emotions.

5. **Seeking Support**:
    - **Therapy and Counseling**: Seek therapy or counseling to address underlying emotional and psychological issues that contribute to gambling behavior. A therapist can help you develop coping strategies and build resilience.
    - **Support Groups**: Join support groups for individuals recovering from gambling addiction. Sharing experiences and learning from others can provide valuable insights and encouragement.
    - **Financial Counseling**: Consider working with a financial counselor or advisor to develop a personalized financial plan and gain expert guidance on managing your finances.

Avoiding financial triggers involves recognizing the factors that lead to gambling and developing strategies to manage them. By identifying triggers, developing healthy financial habits, managing access to money, replacing gambling with positive activities, and seeking support, you can maintain financial stability and prevent relapse.

Seeking Financial Counseling

Seeking financial counseling can provide valuable guidance and support in managing your finances and achieving financial recovery. Financial counselors and advisors offer expertise in budgeting, debt management, savings, and investment strategies.

1. **Understanding Financial Counseling**:
   - **Role of Financial Counselors**: Financial counselors help individuals develop and implement financial plans, manage debt, and achieve financial goals. They provide education, resources, and support to improve financial literacy and decision-making.
   - **Types of Financial Counseling**: There are various types of financial counseling, including debt counseling, credit counseling, budgeting assistance, and retirement planning. Each type focuses on specific financial needs and goals.

2. **Finding the Right Financial Counselor**:
   - **Research and Referrals**: Research financial counselors and seek referrals from trusted sources, such as family, friends, or professional organizations. Look for counselors with relevant credentials, such as Certified Financial Planner (CFP) or Accredited Financial Counselor (AFC).

- **Evaluating Credentials**: Verify the credentials and qualifications of potential financial counselors. Ensure they have the necessary training, experience, and certification to provide reliable and ethical advice.
- **Assessing Compatibility**: Schedule consultations with potential counselors to assess compatibility. Discuss your financial situation, goals, and expectations to determine if the counselor is a good fit for your needs.

3. **Working with a Financial Counselor**:
   - **Initial Assessment**: During the initial assessment, the financial counselor will review your financial situation, including income, expenses, assets, liabilities, and financial goals. They will help you identify areas for improvement and develop a customized plan.
   - **Developing a Plan**: The financial counselor will work with you to create a comprehensive financial plan that includes budgeting, debt repayment, savings strategies, and long-term financial goals. They will provide tools and resources to support your plan.
   - **Implementing Strategies**: The financial counselor will guide you in implementing the strategies outlined in your plan. This may involve setting up automatic transfers, negotiating with creditors, or establishing new financial habits.

4. **Monitoring and Adjusting the Plan**:
   - **Regular Check-Ins**: Schedule regular check-ins with your financial counselor to review your progress, address challenges, and make adjustments to your plan.

Regular monitoring ensures that you stay on track and adapt to changes in your financial situation.

   - **Ongoing Education**: Engage in ongoing education to improve your financial literacy and decision-making skills. Attend workshops, read books, and access online resources to stay informed about personal finance topics.

5. **Benefits of Financial Counseling**:
   - **Expert Guidance**: Financial counselors provide expert guidance and personalized advice to help you navigate complex financial issues and make informed decisions.
   - **Accountability**: Working with a financial counselor provides accountability and support, helping you stay committed to your financial goals and recovery.
   - **Stress Reduction**: Financial counseling can reduce financial stress by providing clarity, structure, and actionable steps to improve your financial situation.

   Seeking financial counseling offers valuable support and guidance in achieving financial recovery and stability. By understanding the role of financial counselors, finding the right counselor, working together to develop and implement a plan, and engaging in ongoing education, you can build a strong foundation for financial well-being.

   Chapter 8 provides a comprehensive exploration of financial recovery and management, including assessing your financial situation, creating a financial plan, avoiding financial triggers, and seeking financial counseling. By actively engaging in these areas,

How to stop gambling by Lucky Willis

individuals can achieve financial stability, rebuild their lives, and support their overall recovery journey.

Chapter 9: Healthy Alternatives to Gambling

One of the most crucial aspects of recovering from gambling addiction is finding healthy alternatives to fill the void left by gambling. Engaging in new hobbies, physical activities, creative outlets, and community service can provide positive, fulfilling, and enriching experiences. This chapter will explore these alternatives in depth, providing detailed guidance on how to incorporate them into your life as part of a sustainable recovery process.

Finding New Hobbies and Interests

Discovering and pursuing new hobbies and interests can play a pivotal role in overcoming gambling addiction. Hobbies not only provide a distraction from gambling urges but also offer a sense of purpose, accomplishment, and enjoyment.

1. **Exploring Different Hobbies**:
   - **Identifying Interests**: Begin by identifying areas that pique your interest. This could be anything from cooking and gardening to reading, photography, or learning a new language. Make a list of activities you've always wanted to try or revisit hobbies you enjoyed in the past.
   - **Researching Options**: Research different hobbies to understand what they involve, the time commitment

required, and any costs associated. Look for local clubs, classes, or online communities that can provide support and resources for your new hobby.
   - **Sampling Activities**: Try out a few different hobbies to see what resonates with you. Attend workshops, take beginner classes, or join introductory sessions to get a feel for each activity before making a commitment.

2. **Incorporating Hobbies into Your Routine**:
   - **Scheduling Time**: Allocate specific times in your schedule for your new hobbies. Treat these time slots as important appointments to ensure consistency and commitment.
   - **Setting Goals**: Set short-term and long-term goals related to your hobbies. For example, if you take up painting, a short-term goal might be to complete a small project each month, while a long-term goal could be to participate in an art show or sell your work.
   - **Tracking Progress**: Keep a journal or log to track your progress and achievements in your new hobbies. Reflecting on your growth and accomplishments can provide motivation and a sense of fulfillment.

3. **Building a Community**:
   - **Joining Clubs and Groups**: Join clubs, groups, or classes related to your hobbies. Being part of a community with shared interests can provide support, encouragement, and social interaction.
   - **Networking with Enthusiasts**: Network with others who share your interests. Attend events, participate in

online forums, and connect with enthusiasts to exchange ideas, tips, and experiences.
   - **Participating in Events**: Get involved in events, exhibitions, or competitions related to your hobbies. These events can provide opportunities to showcase your skills, learn from others, and deepen your engagement with your interests.

4. **Benefits of New Hobbies**:
   - **Stress Reduction**: Engaging in hobbies can reduce stress and provide a relaxing and enjoyable escape from daily pressures.
   - **Personal Growth**: Learning new skills and challenging yourself can lead to personal growth, increased self-confidence, and a sense of accomplishment.
   - **Social Connections**: Hobbies can help you build new friendships and strengthen social connections, which are vital for emotional support and recovery.

Finding and nurturing new hobbies and interests can significantly enhance your quality of life and provide a positive alternative to gambling. By exploring different activities, incorporating them into your routine, building a community, and enjoying the benefits, you can create a fulfilling and balanced life.

Physical Activities and Sports

Physical activities and sports are excellent alternatives to gambling, offering numerous physical, mental, and emotional benefits. Regular exercise and participation in sports can improve your overall well-being, reduce stress, and provide a healthy outlet for energy and emotions.

1. **Exploring Physical Activities**:
   - **Fitness Classes**: Join fitness classes such as yoga, Pilates, aerobics, or spinning. These classes provide structured workouts, expert guidance, and a sense of community.
   - **Outdoor Activities**: Engage in outdoor activities like hiking, biking, running, or walking. Spending time in nature can enhance your mood, reduce stress, and improve your physical health.
   - **Team Sports**: Participate in team sports such as soccer, basketball, volleyball, or softball. Team sports offer the benefits of physical activity along with social interaction, teamwork, and camaraderie.

2. **Incorporating Physical Activities into Your Routine**:
   - **Setting a Schedule**: Establish a regular exercise schedule that fits your lifestyle. Consistency is key to reaping the benefits of physical activity, so aim to incorporate exercise into your daily or weekly routine.
   - **Finding Enjoyable Activities**: Choose activities that you enjoy and look forward to. If you enjoy what

you're doing, you're more likely to stick with it and make it a regular part of your life.
   - **Setting Fitness Goals**: Set realistic and achievable fitness goals. Whether it's running a certain distance, lifting a specific weight, or participating in a race, having goals can keep you motivated and focused.

3. **Benefits of Physical Activities and Sports**:
   - **Physical Health**: Regular physical activity improves cardiovascular health, strengthens muscles and bones, enhances flexibility and balance, and boosts the immune system.
   - **Mental Health**: Exercise releases endorphins, which are natural mood elevators. It can reduce symptoms of anxiety and depression, improve sleep quality, and enhance cognitive function.
   - **Social Interaction**: Participating in sports and group activities fosters social connections, teamwork, and a sense of belonging. Building relationships through physical activity can provide emotional support and encouragement.

4. **Overcoming Barriers to Physical Activity**:
   - **Finding Time**: Make physical activity a priority by scheduling it into your day. Even short bursts of exercise, like a 10-minute walk, can be beneficial if you're pressed for time.
   - **Staying Motivated**: Keep motivation high by varying your activities, setting new goals, and rewarding yourself for achievements. Working out with a friend or

joining a group can also provide accountability and motivation.

   - **Addressing Physical Limitations**: If you have physical limitations or health concerns, consult with a healthcare professional to find suitable activities. Modify exercises as needed to accommodate your abilities and ensure safety.

Physical activities and sports offer a wealth of benefits that can support your recovery journey. By exploring different activities, incorporating them into your routine, and overcoming barriers, you can enjoy improved physical and mental health, social connections, and a positive alternative to gambling.

Creative Outlets

   Engaging in creative outlets can provide a therapeutic and fulfilling alternative to gambling. Creative activities stimulate the mind, promote self-expression, and offer a sense of accomplishment and joy.

1. **Exploring Creative Outlets**:
   - **Art and Crafts**: Try your hand at drawing, painting, sculpting, or other crafts. Art allows you to express emotions, explore your creativity, and produce tangible results.
   - **Music and Dance**: Learn to play a musical instrument, join a choir, or take dance lessons. Music

and dance offer emotional expression, physical movement, and cognitive stimulation.
   - **Writing and Poetry**: Start journaling, writing stories, or composing poetry. Writing can be a powerful tool for self-reflection, emotional release, and creative exploration.

2. **Incorporating Creative Activities into Your Routine**:
   - **Creating a Space**: Set up a dedicated space for your creative activities. This could be a corner of a room, a desk, or even a portable kit that you can take with you.
   - **Scheduling Time**: Allocate regular time slots for creative activities. Consistency helps build a habit and ensures that creativity becomes a regular part of your life.
   - **Joining Classes or Groups**: Enroll in classes or join groups related to your creative interests. Learning from others and sharing your work can enhance your skills and provide motivation.

3. **Benefits of Creative Outlets**:
   - **Emotional Expression**: Creative activities provide a healthy way to express emotions and process feelings. They can serve as a form of therapy, helping to reduce stress and anxiety.
   - **Mental Stimulation**: Engaging in creative pursuits stimulates the brain, enhances cognitive function, and encourages problem-solving and critical thinking.
   - **Sense of Accomplishment**: Completing a creative project brings a sense of pride and accomplishment.

Seeing your ideas come to life can boost self-esteem and confidence.

4. **Overcoming Creative Blocks**:
   - **Finding Inspiration**: Seek inspiration from various sources, such as nature, books, music, or other artists. Inspiration can help spark new ideas and overcome creative blocks.
   - **Starting Small**: Begin with small projects to build confidence and momentum. Small successes can lead to larger, more ambitious projects over time.
   - **Embracing Imperfection**: Accept that not every creative endeavor will be perfect. Embrace mistakes as part of the learning process and focus on the joy of creation rather than perfection.

   Creative outlets provide a rich and rewarding alternative to gambling. By exploring different creative activities, incorporating them into your routine, and embracing the benefits and challenges, you can enrich your life and support your recovery.

Volunteering and Community Service

Volunteering and community service offer meaningful ways to give back, connect with others, and make a positive impact. These activities can provide a sense of purpose, fulfillment, and social connection, all of which are important for recovery.

1. **Exploring Volunteering Opportunities**:

How to stop gambling by Lucky Willis

   - **Local Organizations**: Research local organizations and charities that align with your interests and values. Look for opportunities to volunteer in areas such as animal shelters, food banks, environmental groups, or educational programs.
   - **Community Events**: Participate in community events and initiatives, such as neighborhood cleanups, fundraising events, or cultural festivals. Community events offer a chance to connect with others and contribute to local causes.
   - **Online Volunteering**

: Explore online volunteering opportunities, such as virtual tutoring, mentoring, or contributing to online projects. Online volunteering allows you to make a difference from the comfort of your home.

2. **Incorporating Volunteering into Your Routine**:
   - **Finding the Right Fit**: Choose volunteer opportunities that match your skills, interests, and availability. Finding the right fit ensures that you enjoy the experience and feel valued.
   - **Setting a Schedule**: Commit to a regular volunteer schedule, whether it's weekly, monthly, or for specific events. Consistent volunteering helps build relationships and creates a sense of routine.
   - **Connecting with Others**: Engage with fellow volunteers and staff members. Building connections with others who share your passion for giving back can enhance the experience and provide social support.

3. **Benefits of Volunteering and Community Service**:
   - **Sense of Purpose**: Volunteering provides a sense of purpose and fulfillment by contributing to a cause larger than yourself. It offers an opportunity to make a positive impact and feel connected to the community.
   - **Social Interaction**: Volunteering fosters social connections and builds a sense of community. Working alongside others creates bonds and provides emotional support.
   - **Skill Development**: Volunteering can help you develop new skills and gain experience in different areas. It can also enhance your resume and open doors to new opportunities.

4. **Overcoming Challenges in Volunteering**:
   - **Balancing Commitments**: Ensure that volunteering fits into your overall schedule and doesn't lead to burnout. Balance your commitments to maintain a healthy and manageable routine.
   - **Managing Expectations**: Set realistic expectations for your volunteer work. Understand that not every experience will be perfect, but each contribution is valuable.
   - **Staying Motivated**: Keep motivation high by reflecting on the positive impact of your work. Celebrate the successes and milestones of the organizations you support.

   Volunteering and community service offer enriching and fulfilling alternatives to gambling. By exploring different opportunities, incorporating volunteering into your routine, and enjoying the benefits, you can create a meaningful and purpose-driven life.

Chapter 9 provides comprehensive guidance on healthy alternatives to gambling, including finding new hobbies and interests, engaging in physical activities and sports, exploring creative outlets, and participating in volunteering and community service. By actively incorporating these alternatives into your life, you can create a fulfilling and balanced recovery journey.

Chapter 10: Preventing Relapse

Recovering from gambling addiction is a continuous journey that requires vigilance, dedication, and proactive strategies to maintain progress and prevent relapse. This chapter delves into the intricacies of recognizing the signs of relapse, implementing effective strategies to prevent it, dealing with relapse if it occurs, and learning from setbacks to strengthen your recovery process.

Recognizing the Signs of Relapse

Recognizing the early signs of relapse is crucial for intervening before gambling behavior resumes. Relapse is often a gradual process, characterized by emotional and behavioral changes that precede the actual act of gambling.

1. **Emotional Signs**:
   - **Increased Stress**: Elevated stress levels can be a precursor to relapse. Notice if you feel more overwhelmed, anxious, or irritable than usual.
   - **Emotional Isolation**: Withdrawing from social interactions and activities that you previously enjoyed can indicate a shift towards relapse. Pay attention if you find yourself avoiding friends, family, or support groups.
   - **Negative Emotions**: Persistent feelings of sadness, frustration, or anger may signal an impending relapse. Monitor your emotional state and seek help if negative emotions dominate your thoughts.

2. **Behavioral Signs**:
   - **Neglecting Self-Care**: A decline in self-care practices, such as personal hygiene, healthy eating, and regular exercise, can be a warning sign of relapse. Take note if you start neglecting your well-being.
   - **Resuming Old Patterns**: Reengaging in behaviors or environments associated with gambling, such as visiting casinos or browsing gambling websites, can be a red flag. Be vigilant about any return to old habits.
   - **Lying or Concealing Activities**: If you find yourself lying about your activities or concealing your whereabouts, it could indicate that you're heading towards relapse. Transparency is key in maintaining recovery.

3. **Cognitive Signs**:
   - **Obsessive Thoughts**: Persistent thoughts about gambling or fantasizing about winning can be a precursor to relapse. Be aware of your mental focus and address any gambling-related thoughts.
   - **Rationalizing Gambling**: Justifying or minimizing the consequences of gambling can signal a shift towards relapse. Challenge any thoughts that downplay the risks or rationalize gambling behavior.
   - **Loss of Commitment**: A decline in motivation or commitment to your recovery plan is a significant warning sign. Reassess your goals and reaffirm your dedication to staying gambling-free.

4. **Physical Signs**:

- **Changes in Sleep Patterns**: Difficulty sleeping, insomnia, or excessive sleeping can be indicators of stress and emotional turmoil, which are often linked to relapse.
   - **Health Decline**: Physical health issues, such as headaches, stomach problems, or fatigue, can be connected to emotional stress and may signal a relapse.
   - **Substance Use**: An increase in alcohol or drug use can be a coping mechanism for stress or emotional pain and may indicate a higher risk of relapse.

Recognizing the signs of relapse involves being attuned to your emotional, behavioral, cognitive, and physical state. By monitoring these areas, you can take proactive steps to address any warning signs and prevent relapse.

Strategies to Prevent Relapse

Preventing relapse requires a multifaceted approach that includes building a strong support network, developing coping strategies, maintaining a healthy lifestyle, and staying committed to your recovery goals.

1. **Building a Strong Support Network**:
   - **Connecting with Support Groups**: Join support groups where you can share your experiences, gain insights from others, and receive encouragement. Regular attendance at meetings provides a sense of community and accountability.

- **Engaging with Family and Friends**: Maintain open and honest communication with family and friends who support your recovery. Their understanding and encouragement can be invaluable in preventing relapse.
- **Seeking Professional Support**: Continue therapy or counseling sessions to address ongoing challenges and reinforce coping strategies. Professional guidance helps you stay on track and navigate difficult periods.

2. **Developing Coping Strategies**:
   - **Stress Management**: Implement stress management techniques, such as mindfulness, meditation, or deep breathing exercises. These practices help you stay calm and focused during stressful times.
   - **Healthy Outlets**: Engage in activities that provide positive outlets for your emotions and energy. Hobbies, physical exercise, and creative pursuits offer healthy distractions and reduce the urge to gamble.
   - **Problem-Solving Skills**: Develop problem-solving skills to effectively handle challenges without resorting to gambling. Break down problems into manageable steps and seek solutions proactively.

3. **Maintaining a Healthy Lifestyle**:
   - **Regular Exercise**: Incorporate regular physical activity into your routine. Exercise releases endorphins, improves mood, and reduces stress, making it an essential component of relapse prevention.
   - **Balanced Diet**: Follow a balanced diet that supports physical and mental health. Proper nutrition

enhances energy levels, cognitive function, and emotional stability.
   - **Adequate Sleep**: Prioritize sleep to ensure you're well-rested and capable of managing daily stressors. Establish a regular sleep schedule and create a calming bedtime routine.

4. **Staying Committed to Recovery Goals**:
   - **Setting Goals**: Continually set realistic and achievable recovery goals. These goals keep you focused and provide a sense of direction and purpose.
   - **Regular Reflection**: Reflect regularly on your progress and reaffirm your commitment to recovery. Journaling your thoughts, achievements, and challenges can be a powerful tool for self-awareness.
   - **Celebrating Milestones**: Celebrate recovery milestones, no matter how small. Acknowledging your achievements boosts motivation and reinforces your dedication to staying gambling-free.

Implementing these strategies helps create a resilient and proactive approach to preventing relapse. By building a strong support network, developing coping strategies, maintaining a healthy lifestyle, and staying committed to your recovery goals, you can significantly reduce the risk of relapse.

Dealing with Relapse if it Occurs

Despite your best efforts, relapse may occur. It's important to approach relapse with compassion, understanding, and a plan to get back on track.

1. **Understanding Relapse**:
   - **Relapse as a Learning Opportunity**: View relapse as a part of the recovery process rather than a failure. Use it as an opportunity to learn and grow stronger.
   - **Common Triggers**: Identify the triggers that led to the relapse. Understanding these triggers helps you develop better strategies to avoid or manage them in the future.

2. **Immediate Steps After Relapse**:
   - **Seek Support**: Reach out to your support network immediately. Communicate with family, friends, or support groups to gain encouragement and advice.
   - **Return to Therapy**: Schedule a session with your therapist or counselor to discuss the relapse and develop a plan to address it. Professional guidance is crucial in navigating this challenging time.
   - **Reassess Your Plan**: Review your recovery plan and identify areas that need adjustment. Make necessary changes to strengthen your strategies and prevent future relapses.

3. **Addressing Emotional Impact**:

- **Self-Compassion**: Practice self-compassion and avoid self-blame. Recognize that relapse is common and that you have the strength to overcome it.
- **Emotional Processing**: Allow yourself to process the emotions associated with relapse. Talk about your feelings with trusted individuals and work through any guilt, shame, or disappointment.
- **Positive Affirmations**: Use positive affirmations to rebuild your confidence and reaffirm your commitment to recovery. Remind yourself of your achievements and strengths.

4. **Rebuilding Momentum**:
   - **Set New Goals**: Set new short-term and long-term recovery goals. Having clear objectives provides motivation and direction.
   - **Focus on Small Steps**: Take small, manageable steps to regain momentum. Each small victory reinforces your progress and builds confidence.
   - **Stay Engaged**: Remain actively engaged in your recovery activities, support groups, and therapy sessions. Consistent involvement strengthens your commitment and resilience.

Dealing with relapse requires a compassionate and proactive approach. By understanding relapse, taking immediate steps to seek support and reassess your plan, addressing the emotional impact, and rebuilding momentum, you can overcome relapse and continue your recovery journey.

Learning from Setbacks

Setbacks are an inevitable part of any recovery journey. Learning from these experiences is crucial for growth and long-term success.

1. **Reflecting on Setbacks**:
   - **Honest Reflection**: Take time to reflect honestly on the setback. Analyze what happened, why it happened, and what you can learn from it.
   - **Identifying Patterns**: Look for patterns or recurring themes in your setbacks. Understanding these patterns helps you develop targeted strategies to prevent future setbacks.

2. **Developing Resilience**:
   - **Growth Mindset**: Cultivate a growth mindset that views setbacks as opportunities for learning and growth. Embrace challenges and use them to develop resilience.
   - **Adaptability**: Be adaptable and open to change. Adjust your strategies and approach as needed to better navigate challenges and prevent future setbacks.

3. **Implementing Lessons Learned**:
   - **Adjusting Strategies**: Apply the lessons learned from setbacks to adjust your recovery strategies. Make changes to your plan that address the specific factors that contributed to the setback.
   - **Strengthening Coping Mechanisms**: Enhance your coping mechanisms based on the insights gained

from setbacks. Develop new skills and techniques to better manage triggers and stressors.
   - **Reinforcing Support Systems**: Strengthen your support systems by seeking additional resources or expanding your network. A robust support system provides stability and encouragement during difficult times.

4. **Staying Positive and Persistent**:
   - **Positive Outlook**: Maintain a positive outlook and focus on your progress rather than setbacks. Celebrate your achievements and acknowledge the effort you put into your recovery.
   - **Persistence**: Stay persistent and committed to your recovery goals. Remember that setbacks are temporary and that your determination will lead to long-term success.
   - **Self-Belief**: Believe in your ability to overcome challenges and continue moving forward. Self-belief is a powerful tool in maintaining motivation and resilience.

Learning from setbacks involves honest reflection, developing resilience, implementing lessons learned, and maintaining a positive and persistent attitude. By embracing setbacks as opportunities for growth, you can strengthen your recovery and build a more resilient future.

Chapter 10 provides an in-depth exploration of preventing relapse, including recognizing the signs of relapse, implementing strategies to prevent it, dealing

How to stop gambling by Lucky Willis

with relapse if it occurs, and learning from setbacks. By understanding and addressing these aspects, you can create a robust and proactive approach to maintaining your recovery and achieving long-term success.

Chapter 11: Long-Term Recovery and Maintenance

Long-term recovery from gambling addiction requires a sustained commitment to personal growth, self-improvement, and ongoing maintenance of a healthy lifestyle. This chapter explores the essential elements of maintaining recovery over the long term, including staying committed to recovery, engaging in continual self-improvement, embracing learning and growth, and celebrating milestones along the journey.

Staying Committed to Recovery

Staying committed to recovery is a foundational aspect of long-term success in overcoming gambling addiction. It involves maintaining dedication to your recovery goals, actively participating in support networks, and continually reinforcing healthy habits and behaviors.

1. **Setting Clear Intentions**:
   - **Defining Recovery Goals**: Clarify your long-term and short-term recovery goals. These goals provide direction and purpose, guiding your actions and decisions.
   - **Commitment to Change**: Make a conscious commitment to change and prioritize your recovery journey. Recognize that maintaining recovery requires ongoing effort and dedication.

2. **Engaging in Support Systems**:
   - **Support Groups and Therapy**: Continue participating in support groups, such as Gamblers Anonymous, and attend therapy or counseling sessions regularly. These resources provide encouragement, accountability, and guidance.
   - **Family and Friends**: Maintain open communication with supportive family members and friends. Share your progress, challenges, and achievements with them, and seek their understanding and encouragement.

3. **Developing Coping Strategies**:
   - **Stress Management**: Practice effective stress management techniques, such as mindfulness, meditation, or physical exercise. These strategies help you navigate daily stressors without resorting to gambling.
   - **Identifying Triggers**: Remain vigilant about identifying and managing triggers that could lead to gambling urges. Develop specific coping mechanisms for handling high-risk situations.

4. **Embracing Routine and Structure**:
   - **Healthy Daily Habits**: Establish and maintain healthy daily routines that support your well-being. This includes regular sleep patterns, nutritious meals, physical activity, and meaningful activities.

- **Structured Time Management**: Manage your time effectively to prioritize activities that promote recovery and avoid situations that may jeopardize your progress.

5. **Monitoring Progress and Adjusting Goals**:
   - **Self-Assessment**: Regularly assess your progress in recovery. Reflect on challenges, setbacks, and successes to identify areas for improvement.
   - **Adjusting Strategies**: Modify your recovery strategies as needed based on your experiences and changing circumstances. Remain flexible and adaptable in your approach to recovery.

   Staying committed to recovery involves consistent effort, resilience in the face of challenges, and a proactive approach to maintaining positive changes. By setting clear intentions, engaging in support systems, developing coping strategies, embracing routine, and monitoring your progress, you can strengthen your commitment to long-term recovery from gambling addiction.

Ongoing Self-Improvement

Ongoing self-improvement is integral to sustaining long-term recovery and fostering personal growth. It involves continuously refining skills, cultivating positive habits, and nurturing a mindset of continuous development.

1. **Skills Development**:

- **Identifying Areas for Growth**: Assess areas of your life where you can continue to develop and grow. This may include improving communication skills, financial management, or vocational skills.
   - **Learning Opportunities**: Seek out learning opportunities, such as workshops, courses, or online resources, to enhance your knowledge and skills. Investing in your personal development strengthens your resilience and confidence.

2. **Emotional and Psychological Growth**:
   - **Self-Reflection**: Engage in regular self-reflection to deepen your self-awareness and understanding of your emotions. Journaling or therapy can facilitate this process.
   - **Emotional Regulation**: Practice techniques for managing emotions effectively, such as mindfulness, cognitive-behavioral strategies, or relaxation techniques. Emotional resilience supports your recovery journey.

3. **Building Healthy Relationships**:
   - **Communication Skills**: Enhance your communication skills to foster healthier relationships with family, friends, and colleagues. Effective communication promotes understanding, trust, and support.
   - **Boundary Setting**: Learn to set boundaries in relationships to protect your well-being and maintain healthy dynamics. Boundaries help prevent relapse triggers and promote mutual respect.

4. **Health and Wellness**:
   - **Physical Health**: Prioritize your physical health through regular exercise, balanced nutrition, and adequate sleep. Physical well-being contributes to overall mental and emotional resilience.
   - **Mental Wellness**: Practice self-care activities that promote mental wellness, such as relaxation exercises, hobbies, or engaging in activities that bring joy and fulfillment.

5. **Personal Values and Growth**:
   - **Living in Alignment**: Align your actions and decisions with your personal values and principles. Living authentically supports your sense of purpose and fulfillment in recovery.
   - **Goal Setting**: Continually set new goals and aspirations for personal growth. Goal setting provides motivation and direction, driving ongoing self-improvement.

   Ongoing self-improvement fosters resilience, enhances personal fulfillment, and strengthens your ability to sustain long-term recovery from gambling addiction. By investing in skills development, nurturing emotional growth, building healthy relationships, prioritizing health and wellness, and living in alignment with your values, you cultivate a thriving and resilient recovery journey.

Continual Learning and Growth

Continual learning and growth are essential components of long-term recovery, enabling you to expand your knowledge, embrace new experiences, and evolve personally and professionally.

1. **Embracing Curiosity and Exploration**:
   - **Open-mindedness**: Approach life with an open mind and a willingness to explore new ideas, perspectives, and opportunities. Curiosity fuels personal growth and broadens your understanding of the world.
   - **Lifelong Learning**: Cultivate a habit of lifelong learning by seeking out diverse sources of knowledge. Read books, attend seminars, engage in discussions, and learn from others' experiences.

2. **Adapting to Change**:
   - **Flexibility**: Embrace flexibility and adaptability in response to life's changes and challenges. Resilience enables you to navigate transitions and setbacks effectively, maintaining stability in recovery.
   - **Learning from Adversity**: Extract lessons and insights from adversity and challenges. Each experience offers an opportunity for growth and strengthens your resilience.

3. **Professional Development**:
   - **Career Advancement**: Pursue opportunities for professional development and career advancement.

Enhancing your skills and knowledge can lead to greater job satisfaction and financial stability.
   - **Networking**: Build and nurture professional networks that support your career goals and provide opportunities for growth and mentorship.

4. **Personal Enrichment**:
   - **Cultural Exploration**: Explore cultural activities, travel, and experiences that broaden your perspective and enrich your life. Exposure to diverse cultures and traditions fosters empathy and understanding.
   - **Creative Expression**: Engage in creative pursuits, such as art, music, writing, or theater. Creative expression nurtures self-discovery, emotional expression, and personal fulfillment.

5. **Spiritual Growth**:
   - **Spiritual Exploration**: Explore spirituality and practices that resonate with your beliefs and values. Spiritual growth can provide solace, purpose, and a sense of connection beyond oneself.
   - **Mindfulness and Meditation**: Cultivate mindfulness and incorporate meditation practices into your daily routine. These practices promote inner peace, clarity of mind, and emotional balance.

   Continual learning and growth empower you to embrace new opportunities, deepen your understanding of yourself and the world around you, and maintain a vibrant and fulfilling life in recovery. By fostering curiosity, adapting to change, pursuing professional and personal development, exploring cultural and spiritual dimensions, and integrating mindfulness practices, you cultivate a resilient and evolving recovery journey.

Celebrating Milestones

Celebrating milestones in your recovery journey is a powerful way to acknowledge progress, reinforce positive behaviors, and cultivate a sense of achievement and motivation.

1. **Recognizing Achievements**:
   - **Small Victories**: Acknowledge and celebrate small milestones along your recovery path. These achievements, such as attending support meetings regularly or resisting gambling urges, deserve recognition.
   - **Major Milestones**: Celebrate major milestones, such as weeks, months, or years of sobriety from gambling. These milestones signify significant progress and commitment to your recovery journey.

2. **Reflecting on Progress**:
   - **Self-Reflection**: Reflect on your journey and the progress you've made since beginning your recovery. Journaling or discussing your achievements with others can provide perspective and reinforce your dedication.
   - **Gratitude Practice**: Cultivate a practice of gratitude by acknowledging the positive changes and opportunities that recovery has brought into your life. Express gratitude for the support of loved ones and the strength you've discovered within yourself.

3. **Sharing Successes**:
   - **Community Support**: Share your milestones and successes with your support network, including family, friends, and fellow recovery group members. Their encouragement and celebration amplify the significance of your achievements.
   - **Inspiring Others**: Your journey and milestones can inspire and motivate others who are on a similar path to recovery. Sharing your experiences fosters hope and solidarity within the recovery community.

4. **Rewarding Yourself**:
   - **Personal Rewards**: Treat yourself to meaningful rewards as a symbol of your accomplishments. Choose rewards that align with your values and support your well-being, such as a favorite activity, a special meal, or a relaxing experience.
   - **Avoiding Triggers**: Ensure that your rewards do not involve activities or substances that may pose a risk to your recovery. Opt for healthy and constructive rewards that reinforce positive behaviors.

5. **Setting New Goals**:
   - **Setting Milestone Goals**: Set new milestone goals to continue progressing in your recovery journey. These goals provide direction and motivation, guiding your efforts and encouraging ongoing growth.
   - **Celebrating Future Milestones**: Anticipate and plan for future milestones, knowing that each

achievement reinforces your resilience and commitment to long-term recovery.

Celebrating milestones in your recovery journey strengthens your motivation, reinforces positive behaviors, and fosters a sense of accomplishment and gratitude.

Staying Engaged in Recovery

Staying engaged in your recovery journey requires actively participating in activities and practices that support your well-being and reinforce your commitment to a gambling-free life.

1. **Regular Check-ins**:
   - **Self-Assessment**: Conduct regular self-assessments to evaluate your progress and identify areas for improvement. This involves reflecting on your thoughts, emotions, and behaviors to ensure alignment with your recovery goals.
   - **Feedback from Others**: Seek feedback from trusted individuals, such as therapists, support group members, or close friends and family. Their insights can provide valuable perspectives on your progress and areas needing attention.

2. **Continued Therapy and Counseling**:
   - **Therapeutic Support**: Maintain ongoing therapy or counseling sessions to address any underlying issues

and receive professional guidance. Regular therapy can help you navigate challenges and reinforce healthy coping mechanisms.

   - **Specialized Programs**: Consider enrolling in specialized programs or workshops that focus on addiction recovery, personal growth, or mental health. These programs offer structured support and opportunities for learning.

3. **Support Group Participation**:
   - **Consistent Attendance**: Regularly attend support group meetings, such as Gamblers Anonymous or other recovery groups. Consistent participation provides a sense of community, accountability, and mutual encouragement.
   - **Sharing and Listening**: Actively engage in sharing your experiences and listening to others within the group. This fosters connection, empathy, and a shared sense of purpose.

4. **Healthy Lifestyle Choices**:
   - **Physical Activity**: Incorporate regular physical exercise into your routine. Exercise promotes physical health, reduces stress, and enhances emotional well-being.
   - **Balanced Nutrition**: Follow a balanced diet that supports overall health. Proper nutrition fuels your body and mind, contributing to sustained energy and emotional stability.
   - **Adequate Sleep**: Prioritize adequate sleep to ensure you are well-rested and capable of managing

daily stressors. Establish a regular sleep schedule and create a calming bedtime routine.

5. **Mindfulness and Relaxation**:
   - **Mindfulness Practices**: Integrate mindfulness practices, such as meditation, deep breathing exercises, or yoga, into your daily routine. These practices help you stay present, manage stress, and cultivate inner peace.
   - **Relaxation Techniques**: Explore relaxation techniques that resonate with you, such as progressive muscle relaxation, guided imagery, or aromatherapy. Regular relaxation promotes emotional balance and resilience.

Staying engaged in your recovery involves a multifaceted approach that includes regular self-assessments, continued therapy, active support group participation, healthy lifestyle choices, and mindfulness practices. By integrating these elements into your daily life, you reinforce your commitment to long-term recovery and enhance your overall well-being.

Integrating Self-Improvement Practices

Self-improvement is a continuous journey that involves setting goals, developing new skills, and fostering personal growth. Integrating self-improvement practices into your recovery journey strengthens your resilience and enhances your quality of life.

1. **Goal Setting**:

- **SMART Goals**: Set Specific, Measurable, Achievable, Relevant, and Time-bound (SMART) goals for personal and professional growth. Clear goals provide direction and motivation.
- **Short-term and Long-term Goals**: Establish both short-term and long-term goals to guide your progress. Short-term goals offer immediate focus, while long-term goals provide a broader vision.

2. **Skill Development**:
   - **Learning New Skills**: Identify skills you want to develop or enhance, such as communication, financial management, or vocational skills. Pursue opportunities for learning through courses, workshops, or self-study.
   - **Practicing Consistently**: Dedicate time to practicing new skills regularly. Consistent practice reinforces learning and builds confidence.

3. **Emotional and Mental Health**:
   - **Therapeutic Techniques**: Utilize therapeutic techniques, such as cognitive-behavioral therapy (CBT), to address negative thought patterns and develop healthier coping mechanisms.
   - **Emotional Intelligence**: Work on improving your emotional intelligence by understanding and managing your emotions effectively. This involves self-awareness, self-regulation, empathy, and interpersonal skills.

4. **Healthy Relationships**:
   - **Effective Communication**: Enhance your communication skills to build and maintain healthy

relationships. Practice active listening, assertiveness, and empathy in your interactions.
   - **Boundary Setting**: Learn to set and respect boundaries in your relationships. Healthy boundaries promote mutual respect and protect your well-being.

5. **Personal Growth**:
   - **Self-Reflection**: Engage in regular self-reflection to gain insights into your thoughts, behaviors, and experiences. Journaling or meditation can facilitate this process.
   - **Positive Habits**: Cultivate positive habits that support your personal growth and well-being. This includes practices like gratitude, mindfulness, and self-compassion.

   Integrating self-improvement practices into your recovery journey involves setting clear goals, developing new skills, enhancing emotional and mental health, building healthy relationships, and fostering personal growth. By committing to continuous self-improvement, you strengthen your resilience and create a fulfilling and balanced life in recovery.

Embracing Continual Learning and Growth

Continual learning and growth are essential for maintaining long-term recovery and evolving personally and professionally. Embracing a mindset of lifelong learning enables you to adapt to change, explore new opportunities, and cultivate a rich and meaningful life.

How to stop gambling by Lucky Willis

1. **Curiosity and Exploration**:
   - **Openness to New Ideas**: Foster an open mind and a willingness to explore new ideas, perspectives, and experiences. Curiosity drives learning and personal growth.
   - **Diverse Learning Sources**: Seek knowledge from diverse sources, including books, online courses, workshops, and conversations with others. Diverse perspectives enrich your understanding and foster creativity.

2. **Adaptability and Resilience**:
   - **Embracing Change**: View change as an opportunity for growth rather than a threat. Adaptability enables you to navigate transitions and challenges effectively.
   - **Learning from Experiences**: Reflect on your experiences, both positive and negative, to extract valuable lessons. Each experience offers insights that contribute to your growth and resilience.

3. **Professional Development**:
   - **Career Growth**: Pursue opportunities for professional development and career advancement. This may include additional training, certifications, or networking within your field.
   - **Mentorship and Networking**: Build and maintain professional networks and seek mentorship from experienced individuals. Networking and mentorship provide guidance, support, and opportunities for growth.

4. **Personal Enrichment**:
   - **Cultural and Creative Activities**: Engage in cultural activities, such as attending art exhibits, theater performances, or concerts. Explore creative outlets, such as painting, writing, or music.
   - **Travel and Exploration**: Travel and explore new places to gain exposure to different cultures and experiences. Travel broadens your perspective and enriches your life.

5. **Spiritual and Inner Growth**:
   - **Spiritual Practices**: Explore spiritual practices that resonate with you, such as meditation, prayer, or participation in a spiritual community. Spiritual growth provides a sense of connection and purpose.
   - **Mindfulness and Presence**: Practice mindfulness and cultivate a sense of presence in your daily life. Mindfulness enhances self-awareness, reduces stress, and fosters inner peace.

Embracing continual learning and growth involves cultivating curiosity, adaptability, professional development, personal enrichment, and spiritual growth. By committing to lifelong learning, you enhance your resilience, expand your horizons, and create a vibrant and fulfilling life in recovery.

Celebrating Milestones

Celebrating milestones is a vital aspect of maintaining motivation and acknowledging your progress in recovery. Recognizing and celebrating achievements reinforces positive behaviors and fosters a sense of accomplishment and gratitude.

1. **Acknowledging Achievements**:
   - **Recognizing Progress**: Regularly acknowledge and celebrate your progress, both big and small. Recognize the effort and dedication you have invested in your recovery journey.
   - **Celebrating Milestones**: Mark significant milestones, such as one month, six months, or one year of sobriety from gambling. These milestones signify important achievements and deserve celebration.

2. **Reflecting on Growth**:
   - **Self-Reflection**: Take time to reflect on your journey and the growth you have experienced. Consider journaling about your achievements, challenges, and lessons learned.
   - **Gratitude Practice**: Cultivate a practice of gratitude by acknowledging the positive changes and opportunities that recovery has brought into your life. Express gratitude for the support of loved ones and the strength you have discovered within yourself.

3. **Sharing Successes**:
   - **Community Celebration**: Share your milestones and successes with your support network, including family, friends, and fellow recovery group members. Their encouragement and celebration amplify the significance of your achievements.

- **Inspiring Others**: Your journey and milestones can inspire and motivate others who are on a similar path to recovery. Sharing your experiences fosters hope and solidarity within the recovery community.

4. **Rewarding Yourself**:
   - **Meaningful Rewards**: Treat yourself to meaningful rewards as a symbol of your accomplishments. Choose rewards that align with your values and support your well-being, such as a favorite activity, a special meal, or a relaxing experience.
   - **Healthy Rewards**: Ensure that your rewards do not involve activities or substances that may pose a risk to your recovery. Opt for healthy and constructive rewards that reinforce positive behaviors.

5. **Setting New Goals**:
   - **Continuous Goal Setting**: Continually set new goals to guide your progress and provide motivation. New goals keep

 you focused and committed to ongoing growth and improvement.
   - **Anticipating Future Milestones**: Plan for and anticipate future milestones, knowing that each achievement reinforces your resilience and commitment to long-term recovery.

Celebrating milestones strengthens your motivation, reinforces positive behaviors, and fosters a sense of accomplishment and gratitude. By acknowledging achievements, reflecting on growth, sharing successes, rewarding yourself, and setting new goals, you build a foundation of celebration and growth that supports your continued success in overcoming gambling addiction.

In conclusion, Chapter 11 provides a comprehensive exploration of long-term recovery and maintenance, emphasizing the importance of staying engaged in recovery, integrating self-improvement practices, embracing continual learning and growth, and celebrating milestones. By adopting these strategies, you can sustain long-term success, cultivate personal fulfillment, and build a resilient and thriving life free from gambling addiction. Your commitment to ongoing growth and self-improvement will empower you to overcome challenges, achieve your goals, and maintain a healthy and balanced life in recovery.

Chapter 12: Inspiring Stories of Recovery

Inspiring stories of recovery can provide hope, motivation, and practical insights for those on their own journey to overcome gambling addiction. This chapter shares real-life stories of individuals who have successfully conquered their gambling addiction, the lessons they have learned, and their words of encouragement and advice for others. These narratives highlight the transformative power of perseverance, support, and self-awareness, offering valuable perspectives for anyone striving to achieve long-term recovery.

Real-Life Stories of Overcoming Gambling Addiction

Real-life stories of recovery offer powerful testimony to the resilience and determination of individuals who have battled and overcome gambling addiction. Each story is unique, yet common themes of struggle, redemption, and growth emerge, providing a rich source of inspiration and guidance.

Story 1: Sarah's Journey to Freedom

How to stop gambling by Lucky Willis

Sarah's journey with gambling addiction began innocently enough with occasional trips to the casino. However, what started as a recreational activity quickly escalated into a compulsive behavior that consumed her life. Overwhelmed by mounting debts and strained relationships, Sarah hit rock bottom when she lost her job due to her inability to focus on work.

Determined to reclaim her life, Sarah sought help from a therapist specializing in addiction. Through therapy, she uncovered underlying emotional issues that fueled her gambling behavior, such as low self-esteem and a need for escapism. Joining a support group provided her with a sense of community and accountability. With consistent effort, Sarah developed healthier coping mechanisms, such as journaling and physical exercise, to manage stress and emotions.

Today, Sarah is free from the grip of gambling addiction. She has rebuilt her career, repaired her relationships, and shares her story to help others find hope and healing. Sarah emphasizes the importance of seeking professional help and the transformative power of self-awareness and support.

Story 2: John's Path to Redemption

John's gambling addiction began in his early twenties, fueled by the thrill of winning and the false belief that he could control his luck. His addiction spiraled out of control, leading to financial ruin and the loss of his marriage. Desperate and isolated, John realized he needed to make a change when he found himself contemplating suicide.

John entered a rehabilitation program where he received comprehensive treatment, including therapy, financial counseling, and group support. He learned to identify and manage his triggers, such as stress and boredom, and replaced gambling with constructive activities like volunteering and hiking. Building a strong support network, including reconnecting with family and friends, played a crucial role in his recovery.

Today, John is a passionate advocate for addiction recovery, speaking at events and mentoring others who are struggling. His journey highlights the importance of addressing the root causes of addiction, the value of comprehensive treatment, and the power of community in achieving lasting recovery.

Story 3: Maria's Transformation

Maria's gambling addiction was hidden from her family and friends for years. As a single mother, she felt immense pressure to provide for her children and saw gambling as a way to make quick money. However, her losses far outweighed her winnings, leading to severe financial instability and emotional distress.

Maria reached out to a local support group after a particularly devastating loss that left her unable to pay for basic necessities. The group provided a safe space for her to share her struggles and receive support without judgment. Through the support group, Maria learned about mindfulness techniques and financial management strategies that helped her regain control of her life.

Maria's transformation involved not only overcoming her addiction but also rebuilding her self-worth and confidence. She now works as a counselor, helping others navigate their recovery journeys. Maria's story underscores the importance of seeking help, the benefits of peer support, and the possibility of finding new purpose and direction after addiction.

Lessons Learned from Others

The stories of those who have overcome gambling addiction are rich with lessons that can guide and inspire others on their path to recovery. These lessons highlight the importance of seeking help, embracing change, and fostering resilience.

1. **Seek Professional Help**:
   - **Therapeutic Support**: Engaging with a therapist or counselor who specializes in addiction can provide crucial insights and strategies for managing triggers and underlying issues.
   - **Rehabilitation Programs**: Comprehensive rehabilitation programs offer structured support and

resources for recovery, addressing both the psychological and practical aspects of addiction.

2. **Embrace Community and Support**:
   - **Support Groups**: Joining support groups, such as Gamblers Anonymous, provides a sense of community, accountability, and shared experience. Hearing others' stories can offer hope and reduce feelings of isolation.
   - **Family and Friends**: Reconnecting with supportive family and friends can strengthen your recovery journey. Open communication and honesty build trust and understanding.

3. **Develop Healthy Coping Mechanisms**:
   - **Stress Management**: Identifying healthy ways to manage stress, such as exercise, meditation, or hobbies, can prevent relapse and improve overall well-being.
   - **Emotional Awareness**: Understanding and addressing the emotional triggers behind gambling behavior is essential for long-term recovery. Techniques like journaling and therapy can enhance emotional awareness.

4. **Financial Management**:
   - **Assessing Financial Health**: Taking stock of your financial situation and creating a plan to address debts and manage finances responsibly is crucial for rebuilding stability.
   - **Avoiding Financial Triggers**: Implementing strategies to avoid financial triggers, such as limiting

access to funds or seeking financial counseling, can help prevent relapse.

5. **Commitment to Personal Growth**:
   - **Continual Learning**: Embracing a mindset of continual learning and personal growth fosters resilience and adaptability. Engaging in new activities, pursuing education, and setting goals contribute to a fulfilling life in recovery.
   - **Self-Care**: Prioritizing self-care practices, such as maintaining a healthy lifestyle, practicing mindfulness, and nurturing relationships, supports overall well-being and recovery.

The lessons learned from others who have successfully overcome gambling addiction provide valuable guidance and inspiration. By seeking professional help, embracing community and support, developing healthy coping mechanisms, managing finances responsibly, and committing to personal growth, individuals can build a strong foundation for lasting recovery.

Encouraging Words and Advice

The journey to recovery from gambling addiction is challenging, but it is also filled with opportunities for growth, healing, and transformation. Those who have walked this path offer words of encouragement and advice to help you stay motivated and resilient.

1. **Believe in Yourself**:

How to stop gambling by Lucky Willis

   - **Inner Strength**: Recognize and harness your inner strength. Recovery is a testament to your resilience and determination.
   - **Self-Compassion**: Practice self-compassion and forgive yourself for past mistakes. Every step forward is a victory.

2. **Stay Connected**:
   - **Build a Support Network**: Surround yourself with supportive and understanding individuals. Lean on your support network during challenging times.
   - **Share Your Journey**: Sharing your experiences with others can provide encouragement and foster a sense of community.

3. **Take One Day at a Time**:
   - **Focus on the Present**: Concentrate on making positive choices each day. Recovery is a gradual process, and small steps add up to significant progress.
   - **Celebrate Small Wins**: Acknowledge and celebrate small achievements along the way. Each milestone is a testament to your hard work and dedication.

4. **Embrace Change**:
   - **Adaptability**: Be open to change and willing to adapt your strategies as needed. Flexibility is key to navigating the ups and downs of recovery.
   - **Growth Mindset**: Cultivate a growth mindset by viewing challenges as opportunities for learning and development.

5. **Stay Motivated**:
   - **Set Goals**: Establish clear and achievable goals to stay motivated and focused. Goals provide direction and a sense of purpose.
   - **Find Your Why**: Identify your reasons for wanting to recover and keep them at the forefront of your mind. Your "why" will drive your commitment and perseverance.

6. **Practice Patience and Persistence**:
   - **Patience**: Recovery takes time and effort. Be patient with yourself and the process, and trust that progress will come with persistence.
   - **Persistence**: Stay committed to your recovery journey, even when faced with setbacks. Every effort you make contributes to your overall success.

   Encouraging words and advice from those who have successfully navigated their recovery journey offer valuable insights and motivation. By believing in yourself, staying connected, taking one day at a time, embracing change, staying motivated, and practicing patience and persistence, you can achieve and maintain long-term recovery from gambling addiction.

Your Journey to Recovery

Your journey to recovery is unique, and it begins with a commitment to change and a belief in your ability to overcome gambling addiction. This section provides practical steps and strategies to help you navigate your recovery journey, build resilience, and achieve lasting success.

1. **Acknowledging the Problem**:
   - **Self-Reflection**: Take time to reflect on your gambling behavior and its impact on your life. Acknowledging the problem is the first step toward recovery.
   - **Honesty**: Be honest with yourself and others about your struggles with gambling. Openness and transparency are essential for seeking help and building a support network.

2. **Seeking Help**:
   - **Professional Support**: Reach out to a therapist, counselor, or addiction specialist for professional guidance and support. Professional help can provide tailored strategies for managing your addiction.
   - **Support Groups**: Join support groups, such as Gamblers Anonymous, to connect with others who understand your experiences and can offer encouragement and accountability.

3. **Developing a Recovery Plan**:
   - **Goal Setting**: Set clear and achievable goals for your recovery journey. Outline short-term and long-term goals to provide direction and motivation.
   - **Action Steps**: Develop a concrete action plan that includes specific steps to achieve your goals. This may involve therapy, support group attendance, and lifestyle changes.

4. **Building a Support Network**:
   - **Trusted Individuals**: Identify and connect with trusted individuals who can offer support and encouragement. This may include family, friends, and recovery group members.
   - **Open Communication**: Maintain open and honest communication with your support network. Share your progress, challenges, and achievements.

5. **Managing Triggers and Urges**:
   - **Identify Triggers**: Recognize the triggers that prompt your gambling behavior, such as stress, boredom, or social situations. Understanding your triggers is crucial for managing them effectively.
   - **Coping Strategies**: Develop healthy coping strategies to manage urges and emotions. This may include mindfulness practices, physical activity, and engaging in hobbies.

6. **Financial Management**:
   - **Budgeting**: Create a budget to manage your finances responsibly and prevent financial stress. Set aside funds for essential expenses and savings.
   - **Debt Management**: Address any outstanding debts by developing a repayment plan. Consider seeking financial counseling for additional support.

7. **Embracing Personal Growth**:

- **Learning and Development**: Pursue opportunities for personal growth and learning. This may include education, skill development, and exploring new interests.
- **Self-Care**: Prioritize self-care practices that support your physical, emotional, and mental well-being. Self-care is essential for sustaining long-term recovery.

8. **Celebrating Progress**:
   - **Milestones**: Celebrate your milestones and achievements along the way. Recognize the progress you have made and the effort you have invested in your recovery.
   - **Gratitude**: Practice gratitude by acknowledging the positive changes in your life and the support you have received. Gratitude fosters a positive outlook and resilience.

Your journey to recovery is a path of self-discovery, growth, and transformation. By acknowledging the problem, seeking help, developing a recovery plan, building a support network, managing triggers and urges, managing finances, embracing personal growth, and celebrating progress, you can achieve and maintain long-term recovery from gambling addiction. Remember, recovery is a journey, not a destination, and each step you take brings you closer to a healthier, more fulfilling life.

In conclusion, Chapter 12 shares inspiring stories of recovery, lessons learned from others, encouraging words and advice, and practical steps for your journey to recovery. These narratives and insights provide a wealth

How to stop gambling by Lucky Willis

of inspiration and guidance for anyone striving to overcome gambling addiction. By drawing on the experiences of others, embracing the lessons they have learned, and applying practical strategies, you can navigate your recovery journey with resilience, hope, and determination. Your commitment to change and growth will empower you to overcome challenges, achieve your goals, and build a thriving life free from gambling addiction.

Conclusion

In the final chapter of this book, we bring together all the insights, strategies, and stories shared throughout your journey to recovery from gambling addiction. Reflecting on your progress, envisioning your future, accessing ongoing resources, and finding motivation through final words of encouragement are vital components as you move forward. This chapter aims to consolidate your learning, inspire continued growth, and reinforce your commitment to a life free from gambling addiction.

Reflecting on Your Journey

Reflecting on your journey is an essential step in solidifying your achievements and preparing for future growth. Taking time to look back on the path you've traveled helps to acknowledge your progress, understand the lessons learned, and reinforce your commitment to recovery.

1. Acknowledging Progress:

Reflect on where you started and how far you've come. Consider the initial challenges, the moments of doubt, and the breakthroughs. Acknowledge the small victories and the significant milestones. Each step, no matter how small, represents progress and growth.

2. Understanding Personal Growth:

Examine the changes in your mindset, behavior, and emotional health. How have you developed greater self-awareness, resilience, and coping skills? Recognize the personal growth you've achieved and how it has influenced other areas of your life, such as relationships, work, and overall well-being.

3. Lessons Learned:

Identify the key lessons you've learned throughout your recovery journey. What have you discovered about yourself, your triggers, and your strengths? How have these lessons shaped your approach to challenges and decision-making? Reflecting on these lessons can provide valuable insights for future growth.

4. Overcoming Challenges:

Acknowledge the challenges you've faced and the strategies you've used to overcome them. Reflect on how you managed difficult situations, dealt with setbacks, and persevered through tough times. Recognizing your ability to overcome challenges reinforces your resilience and determination.

5. Celebrating Achievements:

Celebrate your achievements, both big and small. Whether it's reaching a specific milestone, completing a treatment program, or simply maintaining your commitment to recovery, each achievement is worth celebrating. Celebrating reinforces positive behavior and boosts motivation.

Reflecting on your journey allows you to appreciate your progress, understand your growth, and solidify the lessons learned. This reflection serves as a foundation for continued success and personal development.

The Future of Your Recovery

Looking ahead, envisioning the future of your recovery involves setting new goals, maintaining healthy habits, and preparing for potential challenges. This forward-looking approach helps to sustain long-term recovery and ensures continued personal growth.

1. Setting New Goals:

As you progress in your recovery, set new goals that align with your values and aspirations. These goals could be related to personal development, career advancement, relationships, or hobbies. Setting new goals provides direction and motivation, helping you stay focused on your recovery journey.

2. Maintaining Healthy Habits:

Continuing to practice the healthy habits you've developed during your recovery is crucial for long-term success. Whether it's regular exercise, mindfulness, journaling, or engaging in hobbies, maintaining these habits supports your mental, emotional, and physical well-being.

3. Building a Supportive Environment:

Ensure that your environment supports your recovery. This may involve surrounding yourself with positive influences, creating a safe and supportive home environment, and staying connected with your support network. A supportive environment fosters resilience and helps you navigate challenges.

4. Preparing for Challenges:

Anticipate potential challenges and develop strategies to address them. Recognize that setbacks are a natural part of any recovery journey and prepare yourself to handle them constructively. Having a plan in place for managing stress, avoiding triggers, and seeking help when needed can prevent relapse.

5. Embracing Lifelong Learning:

Commit to lifelong learning and personal growth. Continue to seek knowledge, develop new skills, and explore new interests. Lifelong learning keeps you engaged, curious, and motivated, contributing to a fulfilling and balanced life in recovery.

Envisioning the future of your recovery involves setting goals, maintaining healthy habits, building a supportive environment, preparing for challenges, and embracing lifelong learning. This proactive approach ensures sustained success and ongoing personal development.

Final Words of Encouragement

As you conclude this book and continue your recovery journey, it's important to find motivation and encouragement to stay committed and resilient. Here are some final words of encouragement to inspire and support you as you move forward.

1. Believe in Yourself:

You have already demonstrated incredible strength and determination by embarking on your recovery journey. Believe in your ability to overcome challenges and achieve your goals. Trust in your resilience and inner strength.

2. Embrace Hope and Positivity:

Recovery is a journey filled with ups and downs, but maintaining hope and a positive outlook can make a significant difference. Focus on the progress you've made, the possibilities ahead, and the positive changes in your life.

3. Stay Committed to Growth:

Commit to ongoing personal growth and self-improvement. Embrace new opportunities, learn from experiences, and continue to develop healthy habits. Your commitment to growth will sustain your recovery and enrich your life.

4. Seek Support When Needed:

Never hesitate to seek support when you need it. Whether it's reaching out to a friend, joining a support group, or consulting a professional, seeking help is a sign of strength and wisdom. You don't have to face challenges alone.

5. Celebrate Your Achievements:

Take time to celebrate your achievements, both big and small. Acknowledge your progress, reward yourself for your efforts, and take pride in your accomplishments. Celebrating milestones reinforces positive behavior and motivation.

6. Be Patient with Yourself:

Recovery is a gradual process that requires patience and persistence. Be kind to yourself, especially during difficult times. Understand that setbacks are part of the journey and use them as opportunities to learn and grow.

7. Keep Moving Forward:

How to stop gambling by Lucky Willis

Stay focused on your goals and keep moving forward, one step at a time. Each day is an opportunity to make positive choices and reinforce your commitment to recovery. Your determination and perseverance will lead you to a fulfilling and balanced life.

8. Find Joy and Fulfillment:

Seek out activities, relationships, and experiences that bring you joy and fulfillment. Engaging in meaningful and positive pursuits enhances your well-being and supports your recovery.

9. Share Your Journey:

Sharing your recovery journey with others can provide support, inspiration, and encouragement. Whether through writing, speaking, or participating in support groups, your story can make a difference in the lives of others.

10. Remember Your Why:

Keep in mind the reasons why you chose to pursue recovery. Whether it's for your health, relationships, or personal fulfillment, remembering your why will keep you motivated and focused on your journey.

In conclusion, the final chapter of this book emphasizes the importance of reflecting on your journey, envisioning the future of your recovery, accessing ongoing resources, and finding motivation through final

How to stop gambling by Lucky Willis

words of encouragement. Your commitment to recovery, personal growth, and self-improvement will empower you to overcome challenges, achieve your goals, and build a thriving life free from gambling addiction. Remember that you are not alone on this journey, and the support, resources, and encouragement available to you will help you maintain long-term success. Stay resilient, stay hopeful, and continue to move forward with confidence and determination.

I urge you to give your honest review for this book and check out more books by the author most important follow the author for his newly released books

© **Lucky Willis**

www.ingramcontent.com/pod-product-compliance
Lightning Source LLC
Chambersburg PA
CBHW071922210526
45479CB00002B/519